COMMON-SENSE BRIDGE

Rixi Markus

Common-Sense Bridge

Random House

New York

ACKNOWLEDGEMENT

When I wrote *Bid Boldly, Play Safe*, I acknowledged that I could not have done it without the encouragement and help of Derek Senior. When I decided to write this book, I made sure that he would be at my side once again. He will not allow me to say more.

Library of Congress Cataloging in Publication Data
Markus, Rixi.
Common-sense bridge.
1. Bridge whist. I. Title.
GV1281.M3 1973   795.4'15   72-8071
ISBN 0-394-47609-3

Manufactured in the United States of America

CONTENTS

FOREWORD

There are plenty of books about the technique of bridge-playing. Good technique is, of course, essential; but what distinguishes the champion from the good technician is something much more personal—an attitude of mind, a bridge philosophy. I have my own ideas about this aspect of the game, and I am anxious to communicate them, because I believe they can be of value to all aspiring players. But when I came to set down these ideas I soon realised that people with widely differing aptitudes and temperaments would be more likely to benefit from them if I put them in the context of my own development as a bridge player and explained why this game has played so important a part in my life. Then each reader could decide for himself how best to adapt what I have learned to his own situation.

So the time has come for me to look back on my bridge career—to examine why and how it was possible for some-one like me to get to the top almost as soon as I began to play and to stay there for so long. I find it hard to write about myself, but if I am to explain what makes my bridge-mind tick I must first tell my story and then expound my ideas—some are my own and others I have adopted from great masters.

Rixi Markus

PART ONE

BRIDGE AND I

A Player's Story

As long ago as I can remember—and I claim that my memory goes back to the time when I was four years old— my parents and their friends and relations played cards. One of the games they played, called Preference, was distantly related to bridge: there was an auction and a trump suit, but there were only 32 cards. My father and his pals used to play with such concentration that none of them noticed the little girl who was just tall enough to look over the table top, watching them with intense curiosity. I am not sure just when I began to understand the game, but I was soon aware that I might play it better than they did.

My interest in cards was further encouraged by an aunt who lived in the same building in Vienna as we did, and who used to enjoy a game of poker on Saturday nights with her friends. I was sometimes allowed to participate, but of course my parents never knew about this; I don't think they would have approved.

My next step into the card world followed after the end of World War One, when my father discovered that one of his long-lost brothers had made his home in Holland. I was invited to spend holidays with these new-found relations, and the first time I visited them, at the age of ten, I learned to play whist. During my next visit, when I was thirteen, I used to crochet while I watched them play bridge every evening with two friends. One night my uncle said teasingly, 'Pity you can't play; it would break the monotony of this regular foursome.' I looked up at him in surprise: 'Of course I can play.' I then got a lecture about the difficulty of this game I had never played, but I answered defiantly, 'Let me try.' I joined in, and to everyone's amazement I turned out to be the only winner. They wanted to know when and where I had learned the game, but I could not answer, because I had never learned it. I had just watched them play it, and I felt as though I had always understood it. There was nothing about it that puzzled me—except why they played it so badly. Every time they made a mistake it gave me a jolt, like hearing a false note played on the piano.

We played for moderate stakes; nevertheless I returned home with thirty Dutch guilders in winnings. To me this was a fortune and I hid it very well, but my parents eventually discovered it. When I explained the source of my treasure my father was very angry. I had to promise that I would never play cards again, and at first, while I was concentrating on my school work and my music, it was not too difficult to keep that promise.

A few years later I was sent to a finishing school in Dresden where I wrote plays, composed the music for them and produced them; in fact I dreamed of becoming at least a female Max Reinhardt. Both my professor of literature and my music teacher had great hopes that I would attain fame in some direction. One evening a week we were allowed to indulge in any leisure pursuit we fancied, and I recall trying very hard to interest some of the girls in a game of bridge, without much response. On my return to Vienna, however, I found the game had become very fashionable. Bridge clubs were springing up everywhere. Many of my friends and relations were taking lessons and they tried to explain to me what a fascinating game it was, though very difficult to play. When I came out with the assertion that I knew it all, I was met with stony silence. I had a reputation for being honest and truthful, but nobody believed this outrageous statement. 'It takes years to learn to play the game properly,' I was told.

Thus challenged, I was eager to prove my qualifications as a bridge player. By mere chance a young married cousin who, with her Greek husband, had taken up the game with great enthusiasm, introduced me to their bridge circle and very soon I became the bridge prodigy; what I then regarded as 'elderly gentlemen'—professors and famous intellectual figures—stood around and watched me play. Again I was asked where I had learned the game, and I could only reply that I had never 'learned' it. I just knew it, and my standard of play was at least as high as that of the players who made great efforts to absorb the rules and mysteries of the game.

In those days (it was around 1930) we played Plafond Bridge, the forerunner of Contract Bridge. The play of the cards and the defence were exactly the same as today but the bidding and scoring were quite different. We only played rubber bridge, and I knew very little about the competitive game. But slowly tournaments were introduced in Vienna's bridge circles. They were mostly pairs events, and one day one of my regular partners invited me to play in one of these tournaments. He was a lawyer, and as every lawyer in Vienna carried the title of Doctor, he was called Dr Hirschler; a very intelligent and talented player from whom I learned a lot, especially about tactics and attitudes towards competitive bridge. We played an entirely natural system without any conventions, relying mostly on our intuition and flair, and as far as I remember we were always among the first three. People were rather amused at first to see a young girl (I looked much younger than I was) and a fat little man who looked much older playing together, but eventually they learned to treat us with respect.

It was around this time that I met my future husband, who was also much older than I and a very keen bridge player. Although he admired my bridge prowess, he complained bitterly to my father that it was immoral for a young girl to be seen in public surrounded by all those men and attracting so much attention. He simply could not understand how my parents tolerated it. Until then, in fact, my parents had known very little of my bridge life. My father was a very busy man, and I was the middle one of three daughters who all enjoyed his confidence and a great deal of freedom, so I did not think it important to inform him about these activities. However, he summoned me and gave me a lecture, explaining that Herr Markus had told him it was not the right thing for a young lady to be seen in coffee-houses and bridge clubs, and he suggested that I should give it up.

Maybe this was one of the reasons why I married Herr Markus—in order to be able to continue playing bridge, by which I was already so fascinated. The fact that I was such a star performer and enjoyed the adulation of the Vienna bridge community contributed to my eagerness to continue. Not everybody approved of my passion, however. During a school reunion the form-master whom I had idolised remarked coldly, 'So that's what you're doing with your talents. Playing bridge!' as if I had descended to the lowest level of activity. He had set great store by me, and had I not married so young I might well have turned to other fields.

But there was another factor which influenced my new

career. My father had decided for important business reasons to leave Austria and to move to Germany. My eldest sister was then already married and lived in Poland, and as soon as I found out about the impending move I made up my mind that I had to stay in Vienna. I was really in love with the city and I could not face leaving it. I begged my father to allow me to stay with my grandmother and continue my studies, but he was determined that I could stay only if I got married.

When I look back it seems stupid to be in love with a city, but Vienna meant everything to me. I had my friends there; I had my music; I could go to the theatre, which I adored; I had achieved all the things I wanted to achieve there, and without too much effort. I did not take bridge seriously in those days. It amused me; it gave me pleasure and satisfaction; but I could have given it up from one day to the next if necessary. But to give up Vienna seemed impossible to me. So when Herr Markus proposed to me I did not hesitate, and although I was hardly mature enough to realise what it meant, I went into marriage with my usual optimism and enthusiasm.

The shock of disappointment in what proved to be a complete disaster was aggravated by the fact that I found myself pregnant soon after the marriage. At the age of nineteen I had to make up my mind to have a child although I knew that this marriage could not last. I cannot say that I knew it through wisdom or experience; I just knew it through sheer instinct. I could not stay with a person with whom I had nothing in common. I made several efforts for one reason only, that I did not wish to hurt my parents. I was spoilt and immature, but instinctively I knew that I must cling to my bridge life as a drowning person clings to a raft. Through my success as a bridge player I could just bear the failure of my marriage, plus a very grave illness which afflicted me during the last two weeks of my pregnancy and continued for nearly four months afterwards. I was given up as a hopeless case by the leading medical lights of Vienna. Only one of them said, 'You are young; you will live.'

During this illness I was paralysed most of the time, lost my speech and had a day and a night nurse constantly at my bedside. My daughter was taken away to a famous home, where the babies were fed by wet-nurses if their mothers were not able to feed them themselves, and I did not see her until she was nearly four months old. I then had to learn to walk again; for over a year my legs were very weak, and I was allowed very little physical activity. All my dreams of sport or strenuous work faded away. I was told again and again by medical authorities that I would gradually recover some of my strength only if I followed their strict instructions. 'You must do very little, you must be in the open a lot, and just try and relax.' And so I found myself in my favourite city, in the gardens of Vienna's coffee-houses or in the parks, and playing bridge. Fortunately my brain had not suffered (although an embolism in my head had caused great anxiety) and I slowly improved in health.

Whenever I appeared on the bridge scene, I was immediately allocated a place amongst the strongest players, and I was lucky enough to grow up in the same school as Karl Schneider, Hans Jellinek and Elisabeth Klauber. At that time the centre of bridge in Vienna—and especially of national and international bridge competitions—was the Vienna Bridge Club, which had its home at the Grand Hotel, one of the most fashionable in the city and today the home of the Atomic Energy Commission. This was the most exclusive mixed club and the headquarters of the Austrian Bridge League. I knew very little of its existence until Dr Paul Stern, a prominent lawyer and a bridge enthusiast, discovered me playing bridge in one of my regular haunts. He had heard about me, and invited me first to join his club and then to become a member of the future Austrian Ladies' Team. I listened to all he had to say, but I knew that my husband would create difficulties; so I turned to my father, who, after my serious illness and miraculous recovery, could deny me nothing. He was very much aware of my difficulties at home, and spoiled me to a degree which could hardly be equalled. He immediately supported my efforts to turn to competitive bridge as another means of making my married life bearable.

We knew that I could not escape my marriage, because in those days our laws were such that unless both partners were willing to part, there was no way out. I could have run away, but where to, and how, when I was physically frail and had no profession? So I took to bridge as some people in such a situation might take to drugs or alcohol. I thought this would bring me fulfilment, happiness, success—all the things which eluded me in my private life. I knew bridge. I did not have to make any special efforts, and it helped me to meet people and make friends. At the club I found people whom I admired greatly, like Walter Herbert, Dr Edouard Frischauer and Ethel Ernst—probably one of the greatest women players of all time.

It might help my readers to understand the general bridge scene of those days if at this point I record a few historical facts. The International Bridge League was the forerunner of the European Bridge League and was founded in 1932 in Holland. During 1932–39 the I.B.L. organised European Championships and one World Championship in 1937 in Budapest. In 1934 the European Championship took place in Vienna (I knew nothing about it) and at a special meeting of the Committee they decided there and then to include a Women's Championship in 1935 at Brussels. It was to be held simultaneously with the Open Championship, and the same hands were to be played in both events. This was explained to me by Dr Paul Stern when we first met in February 1935 during a big pairs event which I won with my regular partner, Dr Hirschler. Dr Stern went on to say, 'We need you, our Austrian Ladies' Team would not be complete without you. You cannot turn me down.' As I expected, my husband, to whom I appealed for permission to join them, would not hear of it. Again I had to call on my father, who agreed to give me all the support I needed, financially and otherwise.

And so I became a member of the Vienna Bridge Club and the Austrian Ladies' Team. I can hardly describe what a wonderful team that was—and not only because we were a team which never lost. We won that European Championship in Brussels; the year afterwards, 1936, we won in Stockholm; and in 1937 we won the World Championship in Budapest. We were preparing to go to Oslo for the next European Championship in 1938 when Hitler interrupted our ambitious dreams.

At that historically tragic moment we were playing a bridge match at our club. Till then we Austrians had lived in a fool's paradise; most of us did not notice the dangerous clouds darkening the horizon; the Western powers would protect us from the Fascist menace. All we longed for was to become a tourist centre like Switzerland, concentrating on music, offering beautiful scenery and Vienna with all its attractions. How could we have been so blind? There were others who dreamed of the old splendour of the earlier Austrian Empire. Maybe if Germany took us over, greatness could be achieved again. One felt the growing fascination of the

Hitler idea, particularly when one left Vienna and went into the beautiful countryside, high up to the Tirol and other provinces where most folk had hardly ever seen a Jew. (*'Ein Reich: Ein Volk: Ein Führer.'* One Country: One People: One Leader. A people which would not include any Jewish or non-German subjects.) But in Vienna we noticed little and carried on our pleasant life as if Adolf Hitler did not exist. We were sure that Mussolini would never allow him to cross the frontier and would stop him again as he had in 1934. Little did we know that they would soon do a deal which would seal the fate of the little country with its large capital.

I have always disliked fanatics in any shape or form. How can I ever forget the faces of those who did not welcome the *Anschluss* after that Friday in March 1938? Suddenly, when screams of *'Heil Hitler'* were heard, life stood still for us. We simply refused to believe that it was true. On Sunday we had been promised a plebiscite to decide whether the Austrians wanted to remain independent, and as Hitler was sure that the majority of us would vote for independence, he could not wait any longer. We who had hoped for intervention by the Western powers stood paralysed, hoping, waiting, for what? For miracles. How could the free world allow this rape, this incredible crime? Where were our friends?

My father telephoned me from London. 'What are you waiting for?' he asked. I ran around trying to find the best escape route, and my bridge-mind led me to the logical solution. I had heard of arrests of those who tried to run to the Hungarian and other frontiers. I went to Hapag—the Hamburg American line—and asked a young man (don't forget I was young and pretty), 'Can I travel with my Austrian passport through Germany to England?' He replied, 'You must go to the *SS Oberkommando* in Brauener-strasse.' I looked at him, pleadingly. 'Could you telephone? I would rather not go there.' He understood and phoned. The reply was 'Yes'. I asked for one and a half tickets. 'You need a Belgian transit visa,' I was told.

I went immediately to the Belgian Consul and again I saw desperate faces. I was granted a transit visa and on the Tuesday morning I took my little girl and went to the West-bahnhof. Hitler made his 'triumphant' entry into Vienna at that same moment; my taxi had to make a detour to get to the station.

The train was empty but for one English lady who asked me what had given me the idea of going through Germany. I thought about this for the first time, and replied, 'As all the Germans are busy entering Austria, it occurred to me that I might pass through Germany unnoticed.' When our train arrrived at Passau, the natural frontier between Austria and Germany, a German and an Austrian passport officer entered the compartment and looked at me with surprise. They were not prepared for this situation and agreed to let me go. That morning it had been announced on the radio that travellers were not permitted to take more than 20 DM out of the country according to German law. I had not heard this announcement and the two officials let me keep the 200 Austrian schillings I had when I said simply, 'I don't know what will happen to us, or whether we shall be able to pass the next frontier.'

We went to the dining-car and I felt all had gone so well that I must celebrate, so I recklessly ordered half a bottle of Rhine wine. When we arrived in Ostend, I cried and cried. Until then I had restrained my emotions because I had to remain in control, but now all the strains and tensions of the past few days began to tell.

We boarded the boat which took us to Dover. On our arrival I remembered that my father had told me always to tell the truth to British officials and above all never to attempt to smuggle. Smuggling was a kind of sport on the Continent. To bring in some silk from France or Switzerland and not pay duty was a pleasure and a triumph. But now when the immigration officer questioned me I told him the truth, the whole truth and nothing but the truth. That we had fled from the Nazis, that conditions in Vienna were horrible, that people had already been beaten up, taken to camps and to prisons. That hordes of Austrian S.A. troops were let loose on the Viennese Jews to plunder and use violence for fun—their promised reward for waiting patiently in German camps.

I also told him I had come away without money, but that we had ample means in Vienna. 'What will you live on?' he asked. 'My parents are here and I hope my husband will follow us and find work.' After all that had gone before you can imagine my shock when he said, 'I am sorry, you cannot land. And I must advise you not to attempt to try another frontier. You will never be allowed to enter Britain.' And he put a nasty-looking stamp into my passport and crossed it.

I nearly fainted. 'May I phone my father . . . ?' I asked. My little girl cried. I watched the other people from the boat and saw Austrian and German maids (many of them sent to spy) being let in because they had labour-permits as domestic servants. I went to a phone-box and was pressing the button with trembling hands when a tall bobby put his hand on my shoulder. 'You must go back on the same ship,' he said. 'Your boat is leaving.'

I went. What else could I do? And then the Belgian captain of the boat listened to my story. There were about twenty Austrians who had been turned away. He said, 'You will get in because your parents are there.' 'But I have only a transit visa,' I said. 'Will your people allow us to stay in Belgium?' This kind man said to me, 'Go to the passport officer as soon as you arrive in Ostend. I am sure he will not send you back.' And so it was. I shall never forget his kindness. 'Don't go to Brussels,' he advised me. 'Stay here. It might be more difficult there. I shall give you a visitor's visa until you can get into England.' He would not let me pay. 'Keep your money,' he said. I had very little left. I went to the hotel at the Gare Maritime. It was out of season and most of the other hotels were closed, but this one was open and for some reason which I still cannot explain I booked a suite and then telephoned my father. I will never forget that conversation. It began like this:

Father: 'Why didn't you let us know you were coming?'
Me: 'If I'd known I would get as far as Dover safely I would have let you know, but it was a sheer gamble. I didn't want you to suffer any anxiety.'

In those days Austrians did not require visas to enter Britain, but the day after I left Vienna and the *Anschluss* had become an accepted fact, Austrian passports were declared invalid. Jews were only given a German passport marked with a 'J', and were forbidden to leave the country without special permission. By then (the news reached me fast) many of my friends were in camps, in prisons; some had fled, some had committed suicide.

Within two hours of my phone call to my father, I received a nice sum of money from Antwerp by cable, which enabled me to help the other wretched exiles or at least feed some of them. One young man suddenly started a haemorrhage and we took him into my suite. After the doctor had given instructions I found myself nursing a very sick man, and was later told I had saved his life.

Three long days and nights passed and then my father telephoned and said, 'Take the next boat, you can now come to England.' 'Have you got anything in writing?' I asked. 'No,' he said, 'but an Englishman's word is good enough for me.' And then he reproached me for telling the immigration officer all about the events in Vienna and our future plans. At the Home Office they had shown him a typed copy of the interview I had had with the immigration officer. 'But Papa,' I exclaimed, 'you told me to always tell the truth in England.' I also said that if I wasn't let in at Dover I would run right into the sea. That is exactly how I felt. Nevertheless I went to the hairdresser and then we boarded the same boat once more.

On our arrival in Dover the same immigration officer received me with great courtesy and told me with a smile that my father was expecting me. I smiled back. 'I told you you could not keep me out of Britain.'

I must recall that it was Colonel Wedgewood, M.P., who stood up in the House of Commons and made a wonderful speech on our behalf, saying that England should let in at least those few who had managed to get so far and were asking for asylum, and would be risking their lives if they had to return. You will understand that I have a very soft spot in my heart for Belgium too, for had it not been for that kindly passport officer I might have suffered the fate of those six million others.

I have never held any grudge against the immigration officer, who only did what he thought was his duty when he turned me back from England's shores. A year later, on the same day that I had finally been admitted into England, I was returning from a trip to France with a British travel document and a police registration book which proved my right to reside in this country. On this route the immigration officer worked on the boat, and when he noticed that I was feeling slightly sea-sick he kindly suggested that I should sit down and wait until he had dealt with the other passengers. He then looked at my registration book and noticed from the date that it was a year since I had come to Britain. He asked me in a warm voice, 'Do you feel at home with us?' I burst into tears, and it was then that I realised England had become my new country and my new home.

Today I can look back without pain or bitterness to the wonderful atmosphere and days of friendship which made my pre-war bridge experiences so rich. Dr Edouard Frischauer was my idol and I sincerely believe, as do others, that there will never again be anyone like him. I would also claim that Schneider and Jellinek were the greatest pair ever. It is unusual that two equally brilliant individuals should form such a superb partnership. In most famous pairs you will find that one player is just a little stronger than the other. The only exceptions I know in our times are the Belladonna–Garozzo–Forquet trio. Like them, Schneider and Jellinek played in complete harmony, giving an example of how bridge should be played: with good speed, in a most sporting manner, with never an exchange of words and with perfect behaviour towards each other. The kindness of our bridge friends in Norway enabled Jellinek to find a refuge there in 1938. Even today you find players in Norway who remember him and pay tribute to his qualities as a player and as a human being. When the Germans occupied Norway he was deported with other refugees to Auschwitz, where he suffered the fate of most inmates. We heard of his arrival there through Dr Hans Leist, whose mother reported in one of her last messages: 'Jellinek arrived today.'

Dr Hans Leist was a close friend of Jellinek and Schneider and a great player too.

In the Austrian Ladies' Team there was real friendship. I don't recall any signs of bitchiness or jealousy. I believe that I was the darling of the team; because I was the youngest they spoilt me, but they also respected me and were proud of me. I think it was because we were such a harmonious team that we never found it difficult to win. We were nicknamed 'the Goats'—in German, '*die Ziegen*'—by Dr Stern. He had goat-badges made for us, and although it seems funny today it was a great honour to be allowed to be a 'goat' and wear the badge. We took it all very seriously; we had training sessions regularly and were taught that it was important to have the will to win. We were all friendly and pleasant creatures in ordinary life, but at the bridge table we were aggressive fighters and gave no quarter.

This attitude of mind has remained with me and has often led to misunderstandings. Many people have told me, 'You are such a nice, friendly person when one meets you socially, but at the bridge table one is inclined to hate you.' I have always replied that I don't want to be liked at the bridge table. I am most anxious to make friends in the bridge world, but I am much more interested in being respected and feared at the bridge table than in being liked—frankly because it gives me a great advantage. I divide my opponents into two categories—those whom I find it easy to play against, and those against whom I find it very difficult to succeed. I have a different attitude towards players in the second category.

A small incident at the 1971 *Guardian* Easter Tournament in London gave me great satisfaction. My former Austrian team-mate, Gertie Brunner (now Muhsam), was in London on a visit and played in the mixed event with Prince

Waldeck from Germany. They were playing together for the first time and came second. Although she had been very ill, she still gave a wonderful performance. She had not played competitive bridge for many years, but still there was this spark, this fighting spirit, which players trained in the Vienna school have never lost.

I have fought very hard over the years not to allow bridge to dominate my life, because I am fully aware that it is a game—that its importance should not be exaggerated. But to me it has been of great significance. When I was forced to leave Vienna and arrived as a refugee in England with my little girl and with very little else, I had no profession: I knew how to play bridge, and that was all I knew.

As far as England was concerned, however, that was enough. It opened doors which would otherwise have been closed to me. I met a great number of people and made friends, because even in England my name was known and my reputation had preceded me. I had met many British players and bridge officials during my international appearances. Mr Manning Foster, the Chairman of the British Bridge League at that time, entertained me generously and introduced me to one of the leading mixed bridge clubs in London—Almack's in Savile Row. I had already played there as a visitor in 1937. Soon Dr Paul Stern, Karl Schneider, Mr and Mrs Robert Brunner and Lisl Klauber from my team in Vienna followed me to England. We formed a ladies' team with Kathleen Salmon (now Hardy) and Gillie Grant; and again bridge made my life endurable, my exile less cruel than it would otherwise have been. I scored successes, I won money, and it was all very useful and gratifying.

My first great success in this country came in 1939, when Standish Booker and Peter Elmassian, two pupils of Dr

Stern, paired up with Mrs Brunner and myself, and we achieved the distinction of reaching the final of the Gold Cup. Then war broke out. It took some time before I was classified as a refugee from Nazi oppression and the stigma of 'enemy alien' was removed from me. I was allowed to contribute as a fire-watcher and as a part-time secretary at the British Red Cross. I was still physically frail, but slowly improving. During the war I started divorce proceedings in the High Court in London on the grounds of cruelty. Herr Markus refused to admit being domiciled here, so we were forced to alter the plea and ask for judicial separation, which was granted to me after a battle in the courts that lasted for nearly two years. Nevertheless I found myself getting physically stronger because my emotional difficulties had ceased to exist.

Of course bridge activities during the war were different from those of normal times. On the other hand, there were the long nights of air attacks or expected action when there was nothing else to do but play bridge. We then made an effort to form a war team. Leslie Dodds, Graham Mathieson, Eddie Rayne (who because of his bad eyesight was not accepted for active service) and eventually my close friend, the late Walter Carr, son of Sir Emsley Carr, were members. I also joined the Hamilton Club, which had just come into existence at the outbreak of war. Colonel Beasley, one of the most charming bridge personalities, ran the club very efficiently; he welcomed me with open arms and we developed a great friendship. Unfortunately I met him at a time when he was already ailing, but he must have been an outstanding figure in British bridge in his heyday.

I also met Lady Rhodes and found her a most accomplished player. I enjoyed playing with her, so when the war came to an end and bridge life started to become more normal, I formed a partnership with her. It took quite a while before I became a British subject, and until then I was not qualified to play for Britain internationally, but in 1951 Lady Rhodes and I joined the British Ladies' Team, which won the European Championship two years running, first in Venice and in 1952 in Ireland. For various reasons I withdrew after our team had visited the United States in 1953, where we beat the American Ladies' Team in two matches. In the third match we were beaten, but Lady Rhodes and I did not take part in this last match as she had to return home. I didn't play again for Britain until 1955 when I began my partnership with Mrs Fritzi Gordon—still today one of the greatest women players in the world.

One of my treasured memories is captaining, and playing in, a team in Monte Carlo in 1954 against formidable opposition from all over the world, including four of the strongest American teams. It was not so surprising that we won, as my team-mates were Kenneth Konstam, Leslie Dodds, Terence Reese, Boris Schapiro and Adam Meredith. I remember that after our victory Reese and Konstam decided, during a game of golf, that they would ask the British selectors to include me in their team for the European Championship at Montreux in 1954. However, they were told that I was indispensable to the Ladies' Team. Oddly enough, I didn't get to Montreux in any capacity. However, I am glad to be able to report that my Monte Carlo team, with Jordanis Pavlides in my place, won that year not only the European Championship but also the coveted World Championship—the Bermuda Bowl—in New York.

I was deeply hurt and upset when I was not included in the British Ladies' Team for Austria (1957). I had made a point of playing in many national competitions and had done extremely well. That year I also took part in several rounds of selections with different partners, and came top on more than one occasion. Nevertheless when it came to the final choice I was passed over by the selectors. How I would have loved to return triumphantly to the city which had disowned me! Maybe some of those responsible for excluding me knew what it would have meant to me. My friends in the international bridge world knew about this, and with the support of the Austrian Bridge League and its president, the late Dr Reithoffer, I was invited to act as tournament director at this championship. The only vote against me on this occasion came from the British delegate. That same year I had for the first time undertaken to train a ladies' team—Mrs Richard, Mrs Durran and Mrs Whittaker. We entered for the Gold Cup and knocked out a seeded team containing A. T. Priday and Jeremy Flint amongst others. We then reached the eight-team final, where we won the consolation Silver Cup.

Aren't we all vain? Some, of course, are vainer than others. I admit to a normal degree of vanity. One of the most memorable events in my bridge life was the moment when the late Baron Robert de Nexon, our beloved president, presented me with a gold medal in Palermo in 1959, at the end of the European Championships. It had been decided that for the first and, alas, the only time votes would be taken from all the players present to choose the best individual players. According to the President, the choice in the ladies' event was practically unanimous, but in the Open there were several contenders. Jan ('Fat Boy') Wohlin of Sweden won, and he and I were invited as a pair to Denmark the same year. My medal reads: 'To Rixi Markus, the best Ladies' Player at the European Championship: Palermo 1959. E.B.L.'

My other gold medal, which also means a lot to me, is

from Benito Garozzo and reads: 'To Rixi Markus, a perfect partner: Benito, Deauville, 1964.' We played there for the first time together, and won easily.

In 1959 I formed a new partnership with Mrs Whittaker and we brought home the trophy from Palermo. Our team's next triumph was in 1961 in Torquay, when I returned to my partnership with Mrs Gordon. She and I then scored a double success during the Olympiads in Cannes in 1962, when we won the Ladies' Pairs Championship and the Mixed World Championship of teams of four against the strongest world opposition; Mrs Gordon was partnered by Boris Schapiro and Nico Gardner was my partner. A remarkable feature of this event was that I had never before played with Mr Gardner, and we got on like a house on fire. At that time the word went round that Mrs Gordon and I were probably the strongest women's pair in the world. Of course in bridge, as in most sports, current form plays an important part, but we were certainly going strong then.

In 1963 our team won the European Cup in Baden-Baden, and in 1964 the same team scored its greatest success, winning the Olympiad in New York against very stiff opposition, especially from the American ladies. The word went round that the American ladies came second only because they could muster but one ex-Austrian in their team! In 1965 we had some team changes again, and Miss Shanahan became my partner; Mrs Priday (then Mrs Juan) played with Mrs Durran, and Mrs Williams and Mrs Fox completed our team. The Championship took place in Ostend. This was a new team with three new partnerships; nevertheless we were runners-up and only missed the title by one Victory Point.

In 1966 Mrs Gordon and I played together again. We went to Poland and again our team won the title for Britain.

In 1968 we did not participate in the Olympiads because of the Reese/Schapiro affair. The World Bridge Federation had made it clear that they would not accept a British entry with Reese or Schapiro in it, and our Bridge Federation quite rightly decided that we would not participate, because Reese and Schapiro had been cleared by the Foster Tribunal of the allegations made in Buenos Aires and had never been barred from playing in Europe. It was generally accepted that we could have successfully defended our title in 1968 because we then had the strongest team available.

In 1969 we were robbed of victory in Oslo by the inefficient and ludicrous handling of a technical offence. In fact we had been officially declared winners, and the results had been posted on the notice-board, when *the following morning*, if you please, a protest was handed to the Tournament Committee concerning late play in one room during the *first* half of our last match. At the halfway stage in the match we had been told there was no fine, and the table in question had been given the all-clear by the Norwegian Tournament Director. But after the protest the next morning, we were fined two Victory Points, and after further protests and counter-protests an unheard-of official decision was reached—that there would be no Ladies' European Champions that year, and no title. Imagine my surprise, therefore, when in Estoril in 1970 I saw that the French ladies were described in the official programme as the European Champions for 1969.

The 1970 Olympics were both a great triumph and a bitter disappointment. In both the Ladies' Pairs (with Mrs Gordon) and the Mixed Pairs (with George Catzeflis) I was leading all the way, and then my partner and I got pipped at the post. Of course I am very proud to have done so well in such strong fields, but we so nearly. . . . I have now officially asked to be withdrawn as a candidate for the British Ladies' Team. I am happy to have been able to contribute to some of its victories and achievements and will gladly support it in the future in any other way.

So that is the official championship scene; but I have also enjoyed many exciting thrills and spills on the merry-go-round of the Continental grand bridge tour. A successful 1966 Beirut tournament, winning the Pairs with Mrs Gordon and the Mixed Pairs with Benito Garozzo; being narrowly beaten by Garozzo, Yallouze, Sharif and Gresh with my ladies' team (Princess de Liechtenstein, Mme Pouldjean and Mrs Gordon); the Life Masters' Trophy for the best general performance at Deauville, where I repeated the successes of Beirut with the same partners; first place in the Individual and the Open Pairs with George Catzeflis in Israel in 1971—these are just a few of the highlights.

As a result of several incidents in Oslo our team was broken up, and we went to Estoril with two newly formed partnerships which had not been tried out enough. It was easily predictable that the teams which were relying on more experienced partnerships would overtake us, but I knew when I went to Estoril that this would be my final appearance as a competitor in the British Ladies' Team, because I had been making great changes in my bridge life.

During my bridge travels I have formed many new ties, and although bridge and travel go together very pleasantly, I have succeeded in keeping a few weeks every year free of any bridge activity. I still love my music, although I am not a performer, and manage to spend some time every year at the Salzburg Music Festival. I own some wonderful records and have many friends—not necessarily bridge players— who share my interests. I am also crazy about skiing, which I find a challenge because I only started to be physically active again a few years ago. Considering my age and the physical handicaps from which I still sometimes suffer, I do very well. I now ski twice a year—in December and January at St Moritz, and in March at Crans-sur-Sierre, and I believe it helps me and gives me a lot of strength, which enables me to carry on for the rest of the year. I also enjoy swimming and have been told it is good for me.

I think I should emphasise here that it is only because of my success at the bridge table that I am in the fortunate position of being able to afford to indulge in all these other activities. So when I now look back and account for what I did and what I missed, I am convinced I would alter very little if I were given the chance. Of course I made mistakes; I made enemies as well as friends; but all this was part of a rich life. Although there were disasters and even tragedies, they at least taught me to be courageous.

My courage and aggressiveness at the bridge table have often been praised and criticised, but on the whole the balance is in my favour. I have set out to prove certain theories to myself and to the world—that you can play with different partners, with different systems, with more or fewer conventional bids, and still succeed. As long as you use your brain and control your impulses and temperament, you should come out ahead. In itself, a lively temperament can be an advantage, but like atomic energy, you must use it to good purpose.

I have lost count of my trophies and prizes, but I think I can claim to have achieved more in this direction than anyone else anywhere in the bridge world. At one time I resented it when people called me 'Rixi Markus, the bridge player': I did not like to be labelled. But finally I realised that this was what I knew best, and therefore why not?

Then I began to write for the *Guardian*. It was through

John Beavan (now Lord Ardwick), then London editor of the *Guardian*, that I got the job. I was nervous at first but my good friends John Beavan, Harold Lever and Harrison-Gray encouraged me. I listened and learned, and was not ashamed to ask for help and advice. I was also fortunate that Derek Senior was appointed editor of my *Guardian* column. We became good friends and he took a lot of trouble with my articles. He also assisted me in the same manner when I wrote my first book, *Bid Boldly, Play Safe*. He has a special talent for finding perfect titles for my bridge pieces. I am always pleasantly surprised when I open the *Guardian* and read the title he has given my article.

Lord Ardwick recently told me something I had never heard before. After a few weeks had passed since I'd started to write my column for the *Guardian*, the editor, A. P. Wadsworth, said to him, 'The bridge column is extremely intellectual.' I get many letters from readers: most of them give me great pleasure—even those which are meant to criticise—and I answer them all. Now I would like to pass on what I know to some future championship players; I could never teach beginners, but I know I could be a first-class trainer and bring out the best in developing talents. I have informed the British Bridge League that I wish to retire as a player in international ladies' championships, but that my services are otherwise at the disposal of the country which gave me refuge. It was, however, the Portuguese Bridge Federation that engaged me as trainer and non-playing captain for its Ladies' Team for the European Championship in Athens, 1971.

I take tolerance as well as courage to the bridge table. I tolerate those who like to play the most complicated systems, and I often admit that they can do very well by using them; but this does not convince me that I should use them.

I love money bridge as much as I love competitive bridge, but I am aware that they are two entirely different games, and that pairs competitions differ from team events. I like to think that I have mastered them all. Many will disagree, but I have the evidence: I have won fortunes at rubber bridge (I play it much less now); I have won individual contests under most difficult conditions, and countless pairs and team championships in different formations. I admit that there is such a thing as a run of luck: I have had an incredible one for a very long time, and I shall try not to grumble if it runs out one day. I do not begrudge other people their victories, but I never give up trying. My experience accounts for some of my successes, and my confidence in my own ability helps. I try not to be conceited and I never despise my opponents. On the contrary, I respect them and am always prepared to have a battle of wits at the table.

There was a period in my life—thirteen years of a wonderful relationship with a great man of special qualities and brilliance—during which I neglected bridge to a certain extent. I never gave it up entirely, but when this partnership was dissolved I returned to serious bridge and found the solace I so much needed, especially as I had also lost my mother a year before.

In recent years I have extended my activities as a bridge writer, contributing a regular column to the _Queen_ magazine until it ceased publication, and then being appointed bridge correspondent to _Harper's Bazaar_. I was offered the same job by the _Sunday Telegraph_ when it was first produced, and I was greatly honoured and ready to accept, but when the condition was made that I should leave the _Guardian_, because it was also a national paper, I consulted my friends and decided to stay with the _Guardian_, although the other job would have been much more lucrative. Why?

[33]

Because I value loyalty more than anything else and I have always been well treated by the *Guardian*. I had no reason to quit, and I was fortunate enough to be able to afford to do without the increase in my income. I was happy that I did not have to desert the newspaper which took me on as bridge correspondent when I was a beginner, and it is largely due to my experience as a bridge columnist with the *Guardian* that I am now able to write this book.

My Approach to the Game

'Why do people play bridge?' 'What are the difficulties?' 'How long does one need to play before one can consider oneself a good bridge player?' 'How can I improve my game?' 'Why are there comparatively few players of world class?'

I have no doubt that other leading players are asked these questions as frequently as I am, but it is quite possible that the answers prompted by my experience will be different from theirs.

For example, in answer to the first question I would say: In our modern world, full of tensions and anxieties, we are advised by medical experts that hobbies can be of great help to us in finding peace of mind. Bridge is one of many hobbies which are both stimulating and absorbing, and it is not very difficult to acquire a sufficient knowledge of the game to make playing it most enjoyable. It is a game which helps you to meet people like yourself, who want to fill the same need.

And in answer to the second question: When you have got to the stage where you can sit down and play, you will find that the game is much more complicated than you thought. You cannot become a really good bridge player without a great deal of practice, plus some competitive experience. Each individual will develop differently—it depends partly on talent, and partly on character and temperament. Just as some pupils begin to take an interest in their school studies later than others, so it can happen that some bridge players need more time to master the difficulties of the game. We have an excellent example of this in Jonathan Cansino, who, according to his father, looked like an anti-talent when he started to play and then suddenly became one of our youngest stars.

For some people it may take a long time to grasp the difficulties of bridge; for others, no time at all. Without being immodest I think I can honestly claim that the game of bridge never presented me with any difficulties, unless I met a partner who for some reason was not on the same wave-length as myself. But anybody can achieve a certain standard in bridge as in music. If you take piano lessons, practise regularly and listen to good performers, you cannot help but reach a certain standard in your own performance.

However, you must not underrate the difficulties of the game. You must approach it in a humble way, however clever you may be in other fields. You must accept the fact that there is a lot to learn and a lot to know. You may soon find out that some people of much inferior intellectual prowess may easily overtake you, and you may look inept in comparison with them. Forget your pride and vanity, accept the fact that they have more card-sense than you and that what seems difficult to you comes naturally to them. Once you have acknowledged these facts you will also overcome most of your own difficulties. Accept your fate as a mediocre player trying to improve your game, and half the battle is won.

There are several ways to improve your game. One is to play with players who are better than you are, another to watch a first-class table, and a third to play for stakes so high that it hurts you to lose. I would like to expand on this third point. If you can't afford to lose, you will watch your step and learn to discipline yourself, because without discipline you cannot master the game. You will also learn, sometimes the hard way, to get on with your partner. And you will learn to recognise that you have to lose on some hands and to take the disasters in the right spirit. There are bound to be some bad results *en route* to the good ones.

When it comes to money bridge it is important that you show patience and wisdom while the luck is running against you. Then you will be rewarded by losing the minimum during the bad runs and scoring the maximum on your lucky days. It is easier in competitive bridge, where your opponents sitting in the same positions hold the same cards; all you need to beat them is a congenial partner and, often, co-operation from your enemies. With this combination you should easily score sixty to seventy per cent.

Although it may sound contradictory it is true that to be a good bridge player you must have both courage and discipline. Show courage but don't overdo it, and use your self-restraint whenever it is called for.

Having taken in all this, you may begin to understand why there are so few brilliant stars. Here are the essential ingredients for success at the top: talent, humility, self-restraint, self-confidence, courage, respect for both your partner and your opponents, and, above all, excellent judgement and sound psychology. Logic helps a great deal too: I maintain that most women players lack logic but find in their intuition a useful substitute. Some players have some of these qualities, but very few have them all.

Bridge has, of course, changed a great deal in recent years. From a pleasant pastime for the few, it has become an inexpensive hobby for the many and it is gratifying to see young people taking so lively an interest in it. Several hundred schools take part in the English Bridge Union schools competitions, which are growing more and more popular. Many colleges run classes in bridge and I get a great number of letters from readers of my column telling me how they enjoy the game—how it relaxes them—and asking my advice on how to improve. And you can, and I do, enjoy many bridge holidays in different countries of the world—lots of them with specially reduced hotel and air fares. The Scandinavian countries especially have a large bridge-playing population, but Holland, France and Italy are close behind. Perhaps it is not remarkable, considering their meteoric resurgence in most other things, that the Germans have made such rapid strides since the war; there is now hardly a town in Germany without its bridge club, and every week there is another tournament. There is a special Common Market bridge meeting every year, usually won by Italy or France; perhaps we shall be playing there soon?

Where will you go, then? Spain, Portugal, France, Poland, Rumania, Czechoslovakia, Yugoslavia, Morocco, Israel, Majorca, Lebanon, Austria, Germany, Switzerland, Scandinavia, Ireland? Or further afield—Australia, Hong Kong, South America, U.S.A., Canada, New Zealand, India, Malaysia—or am I preaching to the converted?

Of course, some players become addicts and refuse to do anything else with their lives, forgetting that bridge is only a game and a relaxation; but I suppose that with people of this sort, if it wasn't bridge it would be something else—possibly something more harmful. To most of us bridge is a hobby from which we can learn a lot about life—how to adapt, how to keep our tempers, how to practise discipline, how to understand what is meant by ethics and fair play. Children often think that cheating is just fun and clever, and it is most important, surely, that the ethical side of life should be strongly impressed on them. There are so many lessons to be learned from our game.

And above all, what a blessing for those who can escape loneliness when they come to a time of their life when it is hard to find company, or when they lose their life-partners. Instead of being a burden to others, they find solace in the bridge community, which always welcomes new members whether they be eight or eighty.

When I was young and impudent I thought I knew it all. But I soon found out that we never stop learning: the longer we play the more we find there is to know. We encounter new situations and discover new ideas; this is why bridge fascinates millions of people all over the world, always offering the mind so many problems to which there are so many different solutions.

I like to take the straight and direct way to everyday problems and I take this outlook with me to the bridge table. I look at the other three people around the table who are involved in my game with the same interest that I look at all humankind. Who are they? What are they like? How do their minds work? And how can I tune in to them?

First there is my partner. I have learned by bitter experience that unless you treat your partner as you would a good friend you will not achieve good results. It does not matter how little or how much he knows about the game: it is up to you to make him feel safe and confident in order to get his best game from him. Allow him to take part in the bidding and play, and do not treat him with disdain or indifference even if he is far below your own standard. It is surprising how well even a poor player can play if he gets some encouragement, while a good average player will forget all he knows if he is badly handled.

No less important is your attitude to your opponents. You must respect them and not underrate them, yet make them feel you are on top. For you to go down 500 points unnecessarily on the first hand will boost their morale and encourage them. In team competitions it has often been my experience that we won our matches easily when we started with a few successful boards; once ahead we could keep the opposition demoralised and they went from bad to worse. Therefore I make a special effort not to take stupid risks at the start. A team can only play as well as its opponents allow it to play.

The fewer mistakes you make the better your results must be. But the game of bridge depends on so many factors that it is humanly impossible to play without making some errors. You cannot win unless you attack, and there are times when your attack misfires, or the attacked side replies in force. As in life, you are faced at the bridge table with the task of taking difficult decisions. A player who has not sufficient courage to trust his judgement and take a risk is doomed to failure. His negative attitude may protect him from some disasters but he will never be a winner. If you want to win you must take risks and not avoid decisions.

This is probably why there are so very few women champion players in the world. Women in general tend to lean on their men; it is the man of the family who takes important decisions about business, homes, children's education and so on. I do not know of any other woman who arranged how and where her family should go when the Nazis took over Austria in 1938. Everywhere it was the husband, father or brother who decided, 'We must leave,' and then took the necessary steps. Some succeeded; some were too late; but in my case I simply took my child and went, after my husband had refused to go. I knew I could not stay, because if I had done so I would not have remained silent. Maybe I have a sixth sense which guided me then and which is sometimes with me during my game. I am rarely in doubt as to what I should do. I am sure of my decision and even if it turns out badly in the event I am still convinced that it was the right one.

So here you are, sitting down at the table. Handle your partner with great care and be polite to your opponents, but show no mercy: they are your enemy and you must have the killer instinct in order to survive. Then face events with courage. Don't mourn over what is past. Every hand brings new hope, new chances. And the best motto is: 'If the disaster had not happened the good fortune might not have followed'. It so often follows, like the sun after rain, as long as you believe in it. Yes, you must have faith, as in life. Don't look back; so much lies ahead and there are so many hands to come.

Now the game begins and you are ready with the right spirit and in the right mood. Try and shut everything else out of your mind—I never know what day or time it is when I am playing in a tournament. Once I suddenly noticed that everybody had ordered sandwiches, and I could not understand why they were eating until someone told me it was 10 p.m. At the bridge table I never feel hungry or tired; all I have on my mind are the fifty-two cards.

Yes, this is the next step to success: remember to count to thirteen four times. You hold five spades, four hearts, three diamonds and one club; therefore the other players must have the missing eight spades, nine hearts, ten diamonds and twelve clubs. Listen to the bidding and you will already have some information about the cards held by the other three players. Then one player will become declarer, and his partner's hand will go down after the opening lead. Now you can see thirteen or fourteen more cards so you have only to discover the other twenty-five or twenty-six. After each subsequent trick two of these cards will be accounted for. If you concentrate on counting and accounting for all these cards—even the small ones—you will be very close to becoming a champion. At first it seems hard work, but if you persevere for some time it will become automatic. Counting is of the utmost importance whether you are declarer or defender.

If you undertake to make a contract of 4S you must achieve ten tricks. Before you play to the first trick, even if there is a bare ace in dummy, you must make your plan. You must be a disciplined player if you want to improve your game, and part of this discipline is to plan before playing. When you are used to this procedure you will make fewer fatal mistakes, because those made at trick one are most often the ones that cannot be repaired.

One of my favourite slogans, 'Hope for the best but provide for the worst', is here demonstrated from the European Championships in Estoril. The contract was 4S by South. West led the king of diamonds, dummy went down and this is what I saw:

NORTH	♠	K, 10, 6
	♡	A
	◊	J, 10, x
	♣	K, Q, 10, 8, x, x
SOUTH	♠	A, Q, 8, x
	♡	9, x, x, x, x
	◊	x, x
	♣	A, x

I have to make ten tricks, I realised, and therefore I must not lose more than three tricks. If the spades are divided 3–3 there should be no difficulty, but remember my slogan! The opponents played three rounds of diamonds and I discarded a heart on the third round. East then played a heart.

Here are the four hands:

NORTH	♠	K, 10, 6
	♡	A
	◊	J, 10, x
	♣	K, Q, 10, 8, x, x

WEST	♠	J, x	EAST	♠	9, 7, x, x
	♡	K, J, x		♡	Q, 10, x, x
	◊	A, K, x, x, x		◊	Q, x, x
	♣	J, x, x		♣	9, x

SOUTH	♠	A, Q, 8, x
	♡	9, x, x, x, x
	◊	x, x
	♣	A, x

I cashed the king of spades, led the 6 to my ace, and when the jack fell from West, I led a small spade to the 10. I then crossed to my own hand with the ace of clubs and drew the last trump, and my clubs in dummy were good for heart discards. Thus I made four spades, five clubs and the ace of hearts for ten tricks.

Now let us look at the hand again from a different angle. In the other room our opponents reached 5C (I will never know whether they would have made the same play in 4S), and although this looks on the surface to be a safer contract, careful defence can beat it. Declarer (North) cannot rely on ruffing his losing diamond because the defenders have time to play two rounds of trumps, and provided East keeps four spades and West his J, x, declarer cannot enjoy the long spade in dummy (except by taking an unnatural finesse).

However, defeating contracts requires, in most cases, excellent co-operation from a partnership. Indeed, it is generally recognised that defence is the most difficult part of bridge technique. I would go further and say that it is the one aspect of the game which you can only be taught if you have a flair for it. In this case the defence was not too difficult, but even in top circles mistakes in defence do occur. I can count on my fingers the players who know everything there is to know about this subject. I can compare it to playing the violin: there are many good violinists, but how many Menuhins or Oistrakhs are there? 'What should I lead?' I am asked. Of course there are rules, and usually the bidding guides the opening lead. But you must often find a second and third lead, and also the right discards during the play. A certain amount of competence can be acquired by routine experience and by following your partner's guidance; but 'inspired' defenders simply work it out by counting and making logical use of all the available information to place the missing cards. They listen and watch and count: this is part of their secret. But they also have the gift of co-ordinating all this evidence and coming to the right conclusion. It is a bit like deciphering a code or solving a puzzle with certain given clues.

Here is an example which is not too complicated for an experienced player but teaches a good lesson. North dealt at game all. Now keep in mind the bidding sequence:

NORTH	EAST	SOUTH	WEST
1D	Double	4S	5H
NB	NB	5S	NB
NB	NB		

NORTH
♠ 10, x
♡ J, x
♢ A, K, 9, 8, x, x
♣ A, x, x

EAST
♠ A, 9, x
♡ A, Q, x
♢ 10, x, x
♣ K, x, x, x

You are sitting East and your partner leads a small heart against South's contract of 5S. You win the first trick with the ace of hearts and, bearing in mind that you hold the ace of trumps, you look at the dummy and you now use that part of the brain which contains the department of logic. If declarer has two losing hearts there is nothing to worry about, but if he trumps the second heart and draws trumps he can enjoy all the lovely diamonds. So you must try and prevent him from doing so. After all, your partner has bid to 5H vulnerable, so why should he not hold the queen of clubs? So you play the king of clubs and you beat what looks to be an unbeatable contract. Here are the four hands:

NORTH ♠ 10, x
        ♡ J, x
        ◇ A, K, 9, 8, x, x
        ♣ A, x, x

WEST ♠ x   EAST ♠ A, 9, x
     ♡ K, 10, 9, 8, x, x, x   ♡ A, Q, x
     ◇ J   ◇ 10, x, x
     ♣ Q, 10, 9, x   ♣ K, x, x, x

SOUTH ♠ K, Q, J, 8, x, x, x
        ♡ x
        ◇ Q, x, x
        ♣ J, x

How often do we hear from partner, 'Why did you bid this slam, or game?' And how often are we told, 'You could have beaten that contract.' Such comments are part of the game and one learns early in one's bridge life to defend oneself. Sometimes a counter-attack seems the best defence. A long time ago, a lady partner of mine was playing a 3NT contract, and when she went one down I remained silent, trying to be polite. But when she attacked me with, 'Why did you raise me to 3NT?', I simply said, 'Because you could have made it.' So I suggest that, if you wish to have a happy relationship with your partner, you should refrain from criticising his play after the game is over—even if you are absolutely convinced that you can prove your case. If you run into a very bad trump distribution and go down in a slam contract which ought to be bid, and would normally be made, it will upset you to hear from your partner, 'Did you have to bid this slam?' or 'Why did you gamble on . . . ?'

On the other hand I get very irritated when my partner makes a stupid bid and then says to me, 'You are such a good player I thought you would make it.' Here is an example from an Individual Championship which I won in Tel Aviv in February, 1971. I had to play 3NT with the following hand, dealt by North at game all.

	NORTH	
♠	K, 9, 7, 5	
♡	A, 5, 3	
♢	K, J, 6, 4	
♣	K, 7	

WEST		EAST	
♠	10, 6, 4	♠	A, Q, J, 3
♡	7, 2	♡	K, Q, 10, 4
♢	8, 7, 5, 3, 2	♢	10, 9
♣	9, 6, 5	♣	A, Q, 3

	SOUTH	
♠	8, 2	
♡	J, 9, 8, 6	
♢	A, Q	
♣	J, 10, 8, 4, 2	

Bidding:

NORTH	EAST	SOUTH	WEST
1C[1]	Double	1NT[2]	NB
3NT	NB	NB	NB

[1] I shall never know why so many players prefer this bid to any other.

[2] I always bid 1NT after an informatory double by opponents when weak in one of the major suits, because this makes it more difficult for them to bid or to find the best lead. I was also slightly suspicious of the club bid, holding five clubs myself.

West led the 2 of diamonds. I played small from dummy, East played the 9 and I took the trick with the ace. I had been careful not to show any surprise on seeing dummy's hand. Now I played a small club. East took dummy's king with the ace and played the ace and queen of spades. I took the queen with dummy's king and played a small club, on which East played small. I won the trick and continued with another club. East took this trick with the queen and led a small spade. This was not a very inspired defence. He should have led the king of hearts; I would then have settled for one down, losing two spade tricks, one heart trick and two club tricks. Maybe East was not content with one down—he probably thought he would make two heart tricks. Anyhow he led the 3 of spades to West's 10, I discarded a heart and West now (bless him) continued with a diamond. So I made my queen of diamonds, cashed the clubs, entered dummy with the ace of hearts and scored + 600. But when partner said he would not have bid 3NT with anyone but me, I immediately rebuked him: 'We have no reason to be proud of this top. Had we played in 1NT and scored + 120 we would have achieved an excellent score, and one we should have deserved.'

I do not claim to be modest, but I am not conceited. I have tried to explain to many of my bridge-playing friends that it is necessary to gain confidence in yourself if you wish to improve your performance. I do not believe that I play so much better than everybody else, but I have reason to know that many play much worse than I do, and that is one of the explanations of my successes. I remember my disasters more vividly than my triumphs. I enjoy success, but I no longer feel a deep hurt when I fail, simply because I have so often scored that it seems natural to expect that others should score as well. I am content to be among the first ten pairs when it comes to a 300–400 pairs event, though when I am in luck and in good form, we usually arrive in the first five. This seems quite logical, because if we are in the running

COMMON-SENSE BRIDGE

we try hard to improve our position but don't take stupid
risks, whereas if we are badly placed we try to get into a
respectable position by taking risks, which often result in
pushing us down.

My philosophy at the bridge table and my temperament
have improved with years of experience. I have also learned
to adapt myself to different partners; but I cannot play with
players who are egotistical or unfair in their comments.
Those who never see their mistakes and always blame others
for their errors should, in fact, play independently, not in a
game which is properly called partnership bridge. Just a
minor example: I was sitting North when West dealt at love
all:

```
                 NORTH   ♠  x, x
                         ♡  K, Q, x
                         ♢  10, x, x
                         ♣  K, Q, J, x, x

WEST  ♠ Q, J, 10, x, x         EAST  ♠  x, x
      ♡ A, x                         ♡  J, x, x
      ♢ A, x                         ♢  K, x, x, x, x
      ♣ A, x, x, x                   ♣  x, x, x

                 SOUTH   ♠  A, K, x, x
                         ♡  10, 9, 8, x, x
                         ♢  Q, J, x
                         ♣  x
```

Bidding:

WEST	NORTH	EAST	SOUTH
1S	NB	NB	2H
2S	3H	NB	4H
NB	NB	NB	

Having lost 150 on this deal, my partner promptly told

[48]

me that I should have passed over 2S. He also mumbled, 'I did not want those clubs.' It is true that had I held K, x, x, x, x in diamonds instead of the clubs, we might have had a chance to make our contract, but what I did object to was the criticism of my 3H bid. My partner had looked silly going three down and had tried to blame my bid for his misfortune.

PART TWO

COMMON-SENSE BIDDING

Systems

The more often I encounter complicated artificial systems the more strongly I feel about their futility. What a waste of brain-power! It seems as if people who can speak plain clear English are trying to express themselves in a mixture of sounds which they have to learn and remember, and even then they have to be sure that their listeners have not forgotten what they mean to say. Yet I am told that natural bridge is dying, and that the masses want to play the Sputniks, the Precisions, the Orange Club and so forth. Of course I follow certain methods and I need some gadgets to help me exchange valuable information, but when I look at some of the lists of rules for the various systems it makes me dizzy. I also find they give so much information to the opponents that life is made much too easy for them.

But let us be fair: only those players who are talented and have excellent judgement dare walk without crutches. The many millions who now play bridge might not be able to follow the game at all, or might not enjoy it, if they had not got their 'toys'. I have respect for all the Italian systems when they are played by those great masters whose names are known to us all. These experts have used such systems for many years, mostly with the same regular partners, and they are excellent dummy and defence players: they count their tricks, they watch the discards and they make very few errors. But here is an example where I would gladly bet that a natural system would keep you out of what I consider an inferior contract, although everybody concerned complained that the result was unlucky.

	NORTH	♠ A, 9, x, x	
		♡ A	
		◇ K, x, x	
		♣ A, K, J, 10, 9	

WEST	♠ K, J, x		EAST	♠ x
	♡ Q, J, x, x, x			♡ x, x, x, x, x
	◇ x, x			◇ Q, x, x
	♣ x, x, x			♣ x, x, x, x

	SOUTH	♠ Q, 10, 8, 7, 6
		♡ K, 10
		◇ A, J, 10, x, x
		♣ Q

When you look at the North-South hands you will certainly say 6S must be a very good contract, but I was brought up in a strict and disciplined bridge world, and one of our first slogans was, 'When you have more than one long suit, try and play in a no-trump contract, because you never know which suit is going to break favourably.' South was the dealer, and I suggest the following bidding sequence:

SOUTH	NORTH
1S	3C
3D	3S
4D[1]	4NT
5D	5NT[2]
6D	6NT[3]

¹ Showing the same number of cards in diamonds as in spades.

² Confirming all the other aces and asking for kings.

³ Partner has opened with one ace and one king. If he holds S—K, Q, J, x, x; H—x, x; D—A, Q, x, x, x; C—x, he should bid 7S because I have shown a tremendous hand, but if he holds the king of hearts instead of the king of spades, I would rather be in 6NT.

Another possible sequence:

SOUTH	NORTH
1S	3C
3D	3S
4D	4H
4NT	5S
5NT	6H
6NT	

I prefer this second sequence because South knows that his spade suit is broken and that the rest of his hand could prove more valuable in no-trumps, provided he checks on aces and kings.

The next hand supports my theory that the less you disclose about your hand, the more chance you have of fulfilling your contract:

▷

(L. Tintner)

NORTH	♠	9, 7, 6, 4
	♡	A, K, Q, 10
	◇	10
	♣	Q, J, 10, 5

WEST			EAST		
	♠	A, J, 5		♠	3, 2
	♡	6, 5, 4		♡	J, 8, 7, 2
	◇	9, 8		◇	K, 7, 5, 4, 2
	♣	K, 7, 6, 4, 3		♣	A, 9

(Rixi Markus)

SOUTH	♠	K, Q, 10, 8
	♡	9, 3
	◇	A, Q, J, 6, 3
	♣	8, 2

The bidding in our room in a team event went as follows:

NORTH	EAST	SOUTH	WEST
1H	NB	1S	NB
2S	NB	4S	NB
NB	NB		

In the other room the bidding went as follows:

NORTH	EAST	SOUTH	WEST
1C	NB	1D	NB
1H	NB	1S	NB
2S	NB	3NT	NB
NB	NB		

In my case West led the 9 of diamonds—one can hardly blame him—and I had no difficulty in bringing ten tricks home. The 10 of diamonds held the trick and I discarded both clubs on the hearts, allowing East to win the jack of hearts. East then played a trump but the contract could not be broken. I lost two trump tricks and the jack of hearts for +420. In the other room West led a heart and declarer played well to make eight tricks.

If I choose to play a method which is less complicated or more natural than the general trend in most high bridge circles, it does not mean that I do not respect those great players who have chosen a different path. I am only trying to tell the average bridge community that they should not crowd their brains with too many artificial interpretations, because it will not turn them into master-players—it will only tire them out. But the longer the route to a normal contract the more fun it seems to provide for those who choose it.

I am all for having fun at bridge, and when it comes to weighing the advantages and disadvantages of natural and artificial bridge methods, I believe there is not much in it. A good system in the hands of good players will produce excellent results; the best system practised by poor players will prove useless. The Italian school has produced some wonderful players and they have also developed excellent bidding methods—the Roman Club, the Neapolitan Club, the Arno System and, of course, the Livorno Diamond. Belladonna and Avarelli play Roman; Garozzo and Forquet, Neapolitan; Pabis Ticci and d'Alelio, Arno; and Bianchi and Messina, Livorno. So do many others, but have you ever heard their names mentioned?

Garozzo and Belladonna (at this point in time probably the two greatest players in the world) took part in a tour with a Precision Club team which went to many countries playing exhibition matches using that system. I do not know the system well, therefore I am not entitled to comment on it. I can only say that Belladonna and Garozzo would beat almost any opposition playing any system, because their game is so superior that the system plays a minor part in their success. I do not know why or how they reached 3NT on the following hand, which cropped up during their tour in South Africa—a very keen bridge-playing country which has been trying hard to improve its standard and has made great progress. Benito, sitting South, was declarer in 3NT.

NORTH ♠ A, Q, J, 5
♡ 10, 8, 7
♢ K, 10, 8, 5, 3
♣ K

WEST ♠ 9, 8, 7, 2   EAST ♠ 10, 6
♡ Q, J, 9, 6, 5, 3   ♡ K, 4
♢ Q   ♢ A, 9, 7, 6
♣ A, 7   ♣ 9, 6, 5, 4, 2

SOUTH ♠ K, 4, 3
♡ A, 2
♢ J, 4, 2
♣ Q, J, 10, 8, 3

West led the queen of hearts and East hesitated a few seconds before playing the 4. Declarer was in what seemed a hopeless contract. His only chance seemed to be to find East with king doubleton in hearts, and the slight hesitation did not escape his notice. He took the trick with the ace and played the 3 of clubs. West played small and the king in dummy held the trick. Declarer next played three (!) rounds of spades, finishing in his own hand. By now he had learned that West held four spades and a fair number of hearts. The contract still seemed hopeless, but not for the Italian master. He played the queen of clubs, taken with the ace by West, who played a low heart. East took his trick, and at this stage declarer could count West's hand with four spades, six hearts, two clubs and one diamond. (A void in diamonds was unlikely—and why had East discarded a diamond instead of a club on the third spade when he could see five diamonds in dummy? All this did not escape our friend Garozzo.) This was now the position:

	NORTH	
	♠	Q
	♡	10
	◇	K, 10, 8, 5
	♣	None

WEST				EAST		
♠	9			♠	None
♡	J, 9, 6, 5			♡	None
◇	Q			◇	A, 9, 6
♣	None			♣	9, 6, 5

	SOUTH	
	♠	None
	♡	None
	◇	J, 4, 2
	♣	J, 10, 8

East played a club and Benito finessed the 8. He finally played the 2 of diamonds and thus came to ten tricks where many players might have gone down. Was it luck or skill?

Amazingly enough the skilful player usually gets his fair share of luck as well. Skill and luck seem to go together. The French call this '*présence à la table*'. It is very difficult to play against superior bridge masters: you never know what they have got, but they seem to read your mind like an open book.

Keep It Simple

If you have a lot of spare time, a good memory and a suitable partner, then by all means try out one of these complicated systems—you may find one that suits you. But if you want to play light-hearted bridge to amuse yourself then choose a free style. Any simple method will make the game enjoyable for you and your partners and not cause you any headaches.

I can without hesitation recommend the following bidding principles:

A strong 1NT opening bid (16–18 points) makes a solid base, and you can take it anywhere. 2C for your strongest opening is an artificial bid, of course, but it is necessary to have three types of opening bid to show strength: 2NT natural, containing 21–22 points; 2D, 2H and 2S for strong one-suiter and two-suiter hands; and 2C for a game-going hand containing 23 points or more. Add to this one-of-a-suit/three-of-a-suit non-forcing; e.g.,

NORTH	SOUTH
1S	3S

South's 3S response means just what it says: if you have an opening bid of 1S I think we can make nine tricks; I have about 11 points. And also:

NORTH	SOUTH
1S	2NT

South says: if you have an opening bid of 1S I think I can

make eight tricks in no-trumps—I have about 11 points and stoppers in the other suits.

So take the above ingredients, add gadgets to taste, mix well and top with Blackwood.

As I dislike weak-two bids and weak jump overcalls, I like to punish them whenever I can. There are several methods for dealing with weak-two bids and one of them is to double for penalties, but not without some strength outside: e.g., a double of 2S with S—A, Q, 10, 9; H—A, x; D—x, x, x; C—K, J, x, x, should prove lucrative. You can use either 2NT or 3C for a take-out bid and bid naturally with a good suit. If you use 3C for take-out your 2NT will indicate a desire to play the hand in no-trumps. In fourth position I suggest you use an optional double. I remember the following hand with great satisfaction:

	NORTH	♠	A, Q, 10, 8, 3				
		♡	7, 3, 2				
		◇	10, 4				
		♣	5, 3, 2				
WEST	♠	K, J, 9, 7, 6, 5		EAST	♠	2
	♡	9			♡	K, Q, 6, 4
	◇	5, 3, 2			◇	K, 8, 7, 6
	♣	K, Q, J			♣	A, 7, 6, 4
	SOUTH	♠	4				
		♡	A, J, 10, 8, 5				
		◇	A, Q, J, 9				
		♣	10, 9, 8				

West dealt and North-South were vulnerable.

The bidding:

WEST	NORTH	EAST	SOUTH
2S	NB	NB	Double
NB	NB	NB	

I was pleased in the North position to convert my partner's 'optional' double of the weak-two opening bid into a 'penalty'. I led the 10 of diamonds; the result was disastrous for our opponents. Our own West player had opened 1S (rather thin but distribution provides an excuse for this bid). North-South then played in 3H, but our team-mates defended so well that they went one down. West led the king of clubs; East overtook the third round with the ace and then continued with her fourth club.

Good bidding consists to a great extent of being ready with your next bid. All of us know that when we open the bidding we must have a rebid ready, but responder too must give thought to the future course of the bidding. This is particularly so when making a forcing take-out. Look at this hand for instance:

    ♠ Q, J, x, x, x
    ♡ K, x
    ♢ A, K
    ♣ Q, J, x, x

When partner opens 1S, joy enters your heart and you force with 3C. Or do you? If so, you had better be an experienced pair using cue-bids rather than Blackwood. Suppose partner holds:

    ♠ A, K, x, x, x, x
    ♡ A, Q, J, 10
    ♢ x
    ♣ x, x

He will rebid 3H, and over your 3S he will go lolloping into the old Black, and when you show one ace he will automatically take this to be the ace of clubs. You are going to play this hand in some number of spades, so make your force where you hold control—3D.

Looking ahead can also be valuable when choosing an overcall. This hand came up in rubber bridge; West dealt at game all with North-South 60 below the line.

SOUTH ♠ K, 10, 8, x, x
            ♡ A, K
            ♢ x
            ♣ A, 10, 8, x, x

West opened the bidding with 1D, North passed and East bid 2D. Sitting South with the above hand what do you bid? Double? That's what the South I was watching bid and these were the four hands:

NORTH ♠ Q, 9, x
           ♡ Q, 10, x, x
           ♢ J, x, x
           ♣ K, Q, x

WEST ♠ A, J, x   EAST ♠ x, x
     ♡ 7, x, x, x   ♡ J, 9, 8
     ♢ A, K, Q, x, x   ♢ 10, 9, x, x
     ♣ x   ♣ J, x, x, x

SOUTH ♠ K, 10, 8, x, x
           ♡ A, K
           ♢ x
           ♣ A, 10, 8, x, x

This was the full auction:

WEST	NORTH	EAST	SOUTH
1D	NB	2D	Double
3D	3H	NB	NB
NB			

And bang went another rubber.

A little reasoned thought and South would have found the answer. Obviously a double can run into trouble as it did in the event. 2S is better but what if the opposition carry on with 3D? Then you don't know what to do. But what about 3C? If the opposition press on with 3D, which at the score they most likely will, you can then try 3S.

I always get slightly irritated when someone asks, 'Do you play five-card majors?' When I've got 'em I play 'em; doesn't everybody? What they mean, of course, is: do I have five cards in the suit when I open the bidding with 1S or 1H? I answer that, whenever possible, I always open the bidding with 1S or 1H whether the suit has four or five cards. I dislike the 'prepared' club; 1S has as much pre-emptive value as a weak 1NT and is much more difficult to double for penalties! I remember this hand with gratitude: South dealt with East-West vulnerable.

NORTH ♠ None
♡ x, x, x, x
♢ 10, x, x, x, x, x
♣ x, x, x

WEST ♠ A, Q, J, 9   EAST ♠ 10, 8, 7, x, x
♡ Q, x, x   ♡ A, K, J, x
♢ Q, x   ♢ x
♣ A, 10, 9, x   ♣ Q, J, 8

SOUTH ♠ K, x, x, x
♡ x, x
♢ A, K, J, x
♣ K, x, x

The bidding:

SOUTH	WEST	NORTH	EAST
1S	NB	NB	Double
NB	3NT	NB	NB
NB			

Poor dear partner, regretting that he couldn't lead my suit, set off with a diamond and we collected the first six tricks. This was played in a pairs event and some people reached the slam in spades. No other East-West collected a minus score!

Most people opened 1D on my hand and, of course, there were also the 'prepared' clubbers. 'If you open 1S, what do you bid over 2H?' they ask me. 2NT; is that so bad? To bid at the two level, partner must have at least 9 points, so we would have 23 points between us, which should be enough for 2NT.

When playing with strange partners, either at rubber bridge or in individual competitions, remember these rules:

(1) Keep the bidding simple and never make a bid that can be read two or more ways.

(2) Don't suggest conventions and gadgets to your partner when discussing your system. If he says, 'Stayman?' then you can agree, because if he suggests it he probably knows it, but if you initiate any requests for special conventions, your partner may say yes because he is shy of admitting that he doesn't understand them.

(3) If you are the weaker player of the two, don't push your expert partner into contracts which you would not bid with other players; don't attempt to avoid playing the hand when it is obviously your hand that should be declarer; bid and play naturally.

(4) If you are the stronger player be even more careful not

to make a doubtful bid or double. Don't try to play all the hands yourself. It is much more important that a contract should be played from the natural side, even if your partner is not as competent as you are. What is the use of your superior play when you are facing a hopeless task?

(5) If you want your partner to see your signals don't be mean—make them BIG ones—as long as it doesn't cost a trick. Don't peter with the 3 and follow with the 2 if you can afford something more startling.

Now follows a hand which required excellent judgement but which caused a player of great repute suddenly to show a complete lack of it. East-West were playing the Blue Club system, and West as dealer opened with 1D, because in that system a 1C bid promises a much stronger hand. North passed, East bid 1H, South 1S and West 2C. Now over 2S by North, what should East bid?

In my opinion he should make a justified effort of 2NT. Opponents have intervened but not very strongly, and his hand seems useful. In fact, he chose a bid of 3C instead. South then bid 3S and West doubled. In their system this was not a business double: it showed a maximum 1D opening bid with tricks in clubs, and was really intended to be informative—unless it suited partner to leave it. I maintain that if East had held the same hand but with a *certain* heart trick, then he could have passed the double. However, his values became more and more doubtful as the bidding proceeded, though he was not far short of nine tricks in no-trumps if partner held the right cards. In fact he passed and opponents scored +730.

▷

```
            NORTH  ♠  K, Q, 5
                   ♡  7, 5
                   ◇  J, 10, 6, 5, 3
                   ♣  Q, 8, 4

WEST  ♠  J, 7           EAST  ♠  A, 3
      ♡  10, 3                ♡  K, J, 8, 6, 4
      ◇  A, K, 8, 4         · ◇  Q, 9, 2
      ♣  A, K, 7, 3, 2       ♣  9, 6, 5

            SOUTH  ♠  10, 9, 8, 6, 4, 2
                   ♡  A, Q, 9, 2
                   ◇  7
                   ♣  J, 10
```

My sympathies were entirely with West. Although one can say that there is a case for leaving the double in, the risks are too great; besides, North-South made an excellent partnership and were not likely to take silly risks against a part-score in clubs or diamonds. In fact there was not room for everybody. As you can see now, on normal distribution 5C depends only on a heart finesse, but the North-South bidding should have stopped East-West from getting so high. However, 4C is a reasonable contract.

As West is marked with at least nine cards in the minor suits it is unlikely that North-South will have many losers there, and as I have pointed out, East's heart suit is of doubtful quality. 3S were made because East only produced one trick in defence. So in this case my verdict against him is 'Guilty'.

Pre-empts

You must vary your pre-empts: otherwise they have no effect. If everybody knows the strength and weakness of your pre-empts they can easily take the right counteraction. One should not normally open four in a major suit holding two aces, but what else but 4H can you bid on S—x; H—A, J, 10, 9, 8, 7, 6, 5; D—A, x; C—x, x? Or what else but 4S on S—K, J, 10, 9, 8, 7; H—A; D—A, x, x, x, x; C—x? I may find that many experts disagree on the second hand, but in most cases it pays to open high on unbalanced hands. I could open 1S, but what shall I do on the next round?

Here is a hand from a Ladies' Pairs Championship to show how easily you can be pre-empted into a ridiculous contract.

```
              NORTH   ♠  K, Q, x, x
                      ♡  Q, x, x, x
                      ◇  A, K
                      ♣  A, x, x

WEST   ♠  x, x, x          EAST   ♠  x, x
       ♡  x, x, x, x              ♡  A
       ◇  Q, x, x, x              ◇  J, 10, x, x, x, x, x
       ♣  Q, x                   ♣  K, x, x

              SOUTH   ♠  A, J, 10, 9
                      ♡  K, J, 10, 9
                      ◇  None
                      ♣  J, 10, 9, x, x
```

East opened 3D and South doubled for a take-out. West bid 5D and North promptly fell into the nicely-laid trap and bid 6D. This happened to several pairs, including three British Ladies' pairs. I think North should double. This could be a mere business double—South will leave it in only with a suitable hand: otherwise she is going to bid.

Where South passed over 3D the bidding usually went like this:

EAST	SOUTH	WEST	NORTH
3D	NB	5D	Double
NB	6D	NB	6H
NB	NB	NB	

Funny, but it seems that after a clever pre-empt North-South cannot be saved from reaching an unmakeable slam. The fact seems to be that instead of listening to a pre-empt as a warning, most players get hypnotised and hasten to their doom.

I would never dream of opening anything but 4S on S—A, K, 9, 8, 7, x, x; H—None; D—x; C—Q, 8, x, x, x; but if I had bid 4S, opponents had bid 5H, and my partner had doubled, I would never leave the double in. I would respect opponents' 5H bid.

Here is a good example of how lady-players misjudge certain difficult bidding situations. South dealt at game to East-West.

(Mrs Fox)

NORTH   ♠   J, 10, x
           ♡   K, 8, 7, x
           ♢   10, 9, 8, 7, x
           ♣   A

WEST ♠ None   EAST ♠ Q, x, x
        ♡ A, Q, 10, 9, x, x   ♡ J, x, x
        ♢ A, K, Q, x   ♢ J, x, x
        ♣ K, x, x   ♣ J, 10, 9, x

(Mrs Landy)

SOUTH   ♠   A, K, 9, 8, 7, x, x
           ♡   None
           ♢   x
           ♣   Q, 8, x, x, x

Bidding in room one:

SOUTH	WEST	NORTH	EAST
4S	5H	Double	NB
NB	NB		

North found the most favourable lead for declarer, namely the ace of clubs, but at double-dummy 5H cannot be beaten. Bidding in room two:

SOUTH	WEST	NORTH	EAST
1S	Double	Redouble	2C[1]
4S	5C	5S	NB
NB	Double	NB	NB
Redouble	NB	NB	NB

[1] A most stupid bid.

East neither wishes to play in clubs nor wants a club lead. Mrs Landy and Mrs Fox bid the hands very cleverly and deserved the swing of 18 IMPs (International Match Points) from 5H doubled and made in one room and 5S redoubled in the other room. If you play for West to have a void in spades you can even make 6S.

SCALE OF INTERNATIONAL MATCH POINTS

Difference on board				IMPs
0	–	10	=	0
20	–	40	=	1
50	–	80	=	2
90	–	120	=	3
130	–	160	=	4
170	–	210	=	5
220	–	260	=	6
270	–	310	=	7
320	–	360	=	8
370	–	420	=	9
430	–	490	=	10
500	–	590	=	11
600	–	740	=	12
750	–	890	=	13
900	–	1090	=	14
1100	–	1290	=	15
1300	–	1490	=	16
1500	–	1740	=	17
1750	–	1990	=	18
2000	–	2240	=	19
2250	–	2490	=	20
2500	–	2740	=	21
2750	–	2990	=	22
3000	–	3240	=	23
3250	–	3490	=	24
3500 and		up	=	25

Bidding Passed Hands

One aspect of bidding which has been grossly neglected in the textbooks is this: how do you behave, after passing originally, if partner speaks in third or fourth position? There are no strict rules, unless you play a response of 1NT as a strong bid: this convention is called SNAP—Strong No-Trump After Passing. It is not a bad convention, but it can lead to misunderstandings as it is not easy to know where to go from there.

In 'Chicago' rubber bridge and in competitive bridge it is becoming increasingly common for a player to open light in third or fourth position. In ordinary rubber bridge we are inclined to open light if we have a part-score, though one should not open light if the situation is reversed. The reason is obvious: you may start the ball rolling on a hand that might have been thrown in.

Common-sense bridge would recommend that if you open the bidding on meagre values in third or fourth position, you should preferably bid a suit which you would like your partner to lead, in case the opponents buy the contract. Once you have agreed on this principle your partner will know that the purpose of your bid is to help make the strongest attack. If you hold S—K, Q, J, x; H—Q, x; D—J, 10, 9, 8, x; C—Q, J, open 1S and you will be surprised how well such a bid works. In the first place your left-hand opponent cannot now bid on the one level; and secondly, should opponents outbid you, then in most cases you will certainly prefer a spade lead to a diamond. But if your hand looks like S—J, 9, 8, x, x; H—J, 9, 8; D—A, K, Q, J; C—Q, and especially if partner has passed, open 1D.

How often does it happen that you open 1S and the bidding proceeds:

NORTH	EAST	SOUTH	WEST
NB	NB	1S	1NT
NB	3NT	NB	NB
NB			

NORTH ♠ A, x
♡ x, x, x, x, x
◇ 10, 9, x
♣ x, x, x

WEST ♠ K, Q, 10   EAST ♠ x, x, x
♡ A, Q, 10, x   ♡ K
◇ x, x, x   ◇ x, x, x
♣ A, x, x   ♣ K, J, 10, 9, x, x

SOUTH ♠ J, 9, 8, x, x
♡ J, 9, 8
◇ A, K, Q, J
♣ Q

You might ask: what do you do on South's hand if you have opened 1D and partner makes a response of 2C? Very simple: I choose 2NT as a rebid. My partner must have a pretty good hand to bid 2C after 1D and the rebid of 2NT shows a small hand; it can be passed provided you are playing a strong opening no-trump. But if you play the weak no-trump you must open 1S because you have not got the values to bid 2NT after partner's 2C bid.

Now let us assume that partner bids 1H—and remember that 1H over 1D could be a weak bid, since no response on the one level promises a strong hand. Over 1H you can now bid 1S, and if partner puts you back to 2D it will not be disastrous. Over 1S you have the right values to bid 3S and over 1NT you pass.

The advantages of bidding your best suit in preference to your longest suit outweigh the disadvantages.

Here is a good example of passed-hand bidding. My partner Boris Schapiro and I were the only pair to reach a slam on the hand below, dealt by East at game all:

```
          NORTH  ♠  A, K, J, 9, x
                 ♡  A, K, x, x
                 ♢  x
                 ♣  A, x, x

WEST  ♠  x                    EAST  ♠  Q, 10, 8, x
      ♡  x                          ♡  Q, x
      ♢  K, x, x, x, x              ♢  Q, J, x, x
      ♣  K, J, x, x, x, x          ♣  Q, x, x

          SOUTH  ♠  x, x, x
                 ♡  J, 10, 9, 8, x, x
                 ♢  A, 10, x
                 ♣  x
```

Bidding at our table:

EAST	SOUTH	WEST	NORTH
NB	NB	NB	1S
NB	2H[1]	NB	4C[2]
NB	4D[3]	NB	5H[4]
NB	6H[5]	NB	NB
NB			

[1] The common-sense principle that there is no reason to suppress a six-card suit with an outside ace. If partner's opening bid was weak, 2H will not be a bad contract. I consider 1NT would be an unnatural bid. If you had not passed originally you could either pass 1S or bid 2S: I would bid 2S. And please remember that if you have passed in first or

second position and your partner opens in third or fourth position, he may pass after your response, because he simply may not be able to find a further bid.

² The 4C bid tells partner, 'I am ready to play a game and I like your 2H bid; I am even interested in a slam if you can give me some more useful information.'

³ As 4D does not increase the level of your contract it is quite safe to show the ace and also to indicate a mild interest in a further exchange of information. If South held S—x, x, x; H—Q, J, 10, x, x, x; D—A, x; C—x, x, he should not bid 4D because he cannot expect North to produce enough controls for a slam. Note that the singleton club becomes a vital card as partner has virtually promised you at least the ace in the suit.

⁴ North now hands the buck back to South. He says, 'I am very strong; I do not think we can lose 5H; but you must take the final decision.'

⁵ South gets the message. He decides that he might, at the worst, have to depend on a finesse if the spade holding is K, J, 10, x, x, or A, Q, 10, x, x, but he judges that the odds are in his favour and when he sees dummy he is glad to have taken the decision.

Those who in South's position decided that they could not bid 2H because they 'only had five points', and therefore bid 2S, reached 4S, 5S or 6S. Of course it is unlucky that 6S cannot be made, but 6H is definitely the superior contract.

So let us summarise. It makes a big difference to your bidding whether or not you have already passed. Try and help your partner, and remember that after an original pass no bid you make is forcing—unless you overcall opponents' suit or jump in a side suit after partner has opened one in a major suit.

I avoid opening minor suits whenever possible. The 1C and 1D bidders leave the door wide open for their opponents. How easily I can come in over 1C or 1D to show my partner which suit I want led. For example, I can easily bid 1S or 1H with K, J, 10, 9, 8, and very little else. With S—Q, J, x, x; H—K, x, x; D—A, J, x, x; C—Q, x, I shall always open 1S. With S—J, x, x; H—K, J, 10, x; D—K, x, x, x; C—A, x, I open 1H. With S—10, 9, 8, x, x; H—A, K, Q, J; D—Q, x; C—Q, J, I open 1H. And with S—A, K, J, 10; H—9, x, x, x, x; D—Q, J, x; C—Q, I open 1S.

I object to the weak no-trump because it advertises your weakness to everybody; and how can your partner guess what to lead? When I bid 1H or 1S on a weak hand it acts as a pre-empt; opponents do not yet know whether I am weak or strong, and they may cautiously wait until it becomes too late for them to come in. Of course to succeed you must have an intelligent partner, who will co-operate instead of blocking your path, but this applies to all systems and bidding arrangements.

I know how exact some bidding systems are. My bidding theories leave a lot to the player's imagination and intuition, but my opponents are very often kept in the dark—and believe me it is much more fun. The systems which have invented a bid for practically every type of hand are in fact boring. They are a burden to your memory, and your brain is tired by the time you have to plan your play and defence. I do not wish to prophesy, but I believe that many talented players will eventually discard most of their crutches and make top-class bridge an elegant and intellectual game again, instead of a tortured collection of artificial expressions. At every championship we are handed accurate descriptions of our opponents' systems, usually running to at least two or three pages. My reaction remains the same: poor players!

How tired you must be carrying all this weight around with you, while I remain free to use my brain for the more important task of making tricks in attack and defence!

An intelligent partner will not bid 2C over your 1S with S—J, x; H—x, x, x, x; D—A, J, x; C—K, J, x, x, or 2D over your 1H with S—10, x, x; H—J, x, x; D—K, Q, x, x; C—K, x,x. On both hands he will reply 1NT, which shows a balanced hand. You may feel that with such a hand you are too good for a one-bid, but it is much better to play a part-score and make overtricks than to get too high. After all, if you play the 16–18 or 15–17 no-trump and your partner has not opened 1NT, you know that either he has not got the necessary values or his hand is unbalanced, in which case you will hear from him. You can be as good as S—A, K, x; H—J, x, x, x; D—Q, x, x; C—J, x, x, and still find it quite difficult to make 1NT after partner has opened 1C or 1D. Again, don't bid 1H on such a hand because you may be left there—and do you wish to play 1H opposite a hand like S—x, x; H—Q, x; D—K, J, 10, 9, x; C—A, x, x, x? I could give many examples, but it all boils down to the principle that you must avoid punishing your partner, who is on your side and wishes to indicate a useful lead.

Again and again I have seen it happen that partners who have passed have forgotten that they may be left in whatever bid they make, because there is no forcing situation after an original pass except in the following cases:

(1) if you overcall opponents' suit: e.g.

NORTH	EAST	SOUTH	WEST
NB	NB	1H	1S
2S	NB	?	

South must then find another bid.

(2) if in third or fourth position partner opens 1H or 1S and

you can see that you are close to 4H or 4S; in that case you make a jump in a side suit, which is absolutely forcing for one round. If partner has his proper values for an opening bid he must then bid game or bid a new suit.

Here is an example. Your partner opens 1S in third or fourth position and you hold S—10, 9, 8, x, x; H—Q; D—A, K, x; C—10, 9, x, x. You are too good for 3S and must allow for the possibility that partner has made a weak bid, so you bid 3D and if partner bids 3S you must pass. If you hold S—K, Q, x, x; H—J, x, x, x; D—x, x; C—A, J, x, you bid 3C. Always force when you have tricks and let partner judge from his own hand how useful your hand can be.

Avoid jumping to 2NT even if you hold 11 balanced points: you may be punishing a partner who for some reason has thought it wiser to bid 1S on something like S—K, Q, J, 10, x; H—Q, x; D—J, x, x, x; C—10, x. Many of us think it is essential to open 1S on such a hand in third position, mainly as a lead-directing bid; but if, when you do so, your partner decides that because he passed on 10–11 points he is now entitled to jump the bidding, then your partner is punishing you for a bid which could have been of benefit to you both. If he holds a poorish hand he should be grateful to know what to lead, so if you do bid on a weak hand in third or fourth position, be sure you bid the suit that you want led if the other side plays the hand. I would rather open 1H than 1D on S—Q, J; H—K, Q, J; D—J, 10, 9, x, x; C—Q, x, x after partner has passed, and with an intelligent partner it should not be dangerous.

If your partner makes an optimistic or lead-directing effort after your original pass, remember that you are also on the receiving end, and that your profits and losses are equally shared. Given a good partnership understanding, I am in favour of opening on light values as long as you are prepared for your next bid.

When it comes to competitive bridge it is often essential to open on light hands even in fourth position. I am therefore in favour of using the weak no-trump in fourth position *only*. On the whole I detest the weak no-trump and have often preached against it; nobody can convince me that it is a good weapon; but I do appreciate that, especially in pairs competitions, it can be useful to be able to open on 12–14 points in fourth position without getting your partner so excited that he does not let go before you reach an unmakeable contract. Part-scores can be of great value in rubber bridge, too.

Finally, when you play common-sense bridge you must accept the fact that if you open 1S in third or fourth position, your partner cannot reply 1NT on S—x; H—K, J, 10, 9, x, x; D—x, x, x; C—x, x, x, or on S—Q; H—Q, x, x; D—J, x, x; C—Q, J, 10, 9, 8, x, or on S—x, x; H—J, x; D—K, J, 9, x, x, x; C—J, x, x, and so on. He must be allowed to bid respectively 2H, 2C and 2D, and you must remember that this is *not* forcing; it is simply telling you that his hand is not balanced and that he thinks he can make 2H, 2C or 2D opposite your bid of 1S.

Slams

When I am asked what slam-bidding system I favour I can sincerely say, 'Any system, as long as one makes correct use of it, and as long as one understands how to play.'

You can reach your best contract by various routes, but don't get lost. I look at a hand and I say to myself, 'What is this hand worth?' Here, for example, is one which I am not likely to forget because it probably cost us the Olympic title in the Ladies' Pairs in Stockholm. We were leading comfortably when I picked up S—A; H—Q, J, 10, 8, 6, 5; D—None; C—A, K, 10, 9, 8, 2. I have my own bidding ideas and I consider this hand too good for an opening bid of 1H. We play a Two-Club system. All I need is the queen of clubs or the king of hearts to make a game. Therefore I opened 2H.

Here are the North-South hands and the bidding sequence, with no intervention from East-West.

	NORTH	
	♠	A
	♡	Q, J, 10, 8, 6, 5
	◇	None
	♣	A, K, 10, 9, 8, 2
	SOUTH	
	♠	J, 10, 9, 8, 6, 5
	♡	A, K, 4
	◇	A, 9, 2
	♣	J

NORTH	SOUTH
2H	2S
3C	3D
4C	6H
NB	

My partner knew that I had opened 2H missing the two top honours, and after 3C the 3D bid was futile. 4NT and 5NT would have led easily to 7H, but I would have preferred the bidding to go:

NORTH	SOUTH
2H	3H
5NT[1]	7H
NB	

[1] 5NT is a grand slam force, asking partner to bid 7 with two of the three top honours in the agreed suit.

Fix the suit first, try and give partner the most valuable information as early as possible and then you can use cue-bids, Blackwood and so on. The 2S bid spoilt the sequence, in my opinion. As I often tell my readers, when you have found a fit, why look for a misfit?

And then there was a second hand on which we failed to reach a grand slam:

NORTH ♠ J, 6
♡ A, 10, 9, 6
♢ A, K, J, 10, 9, 5
♣ 9

SOUTH ♠ A, K, Q, 10, 9, 5
♡ 7
♢ 7, 3
♣ A, K, 8, 2

Bidding:

NORTH	SOUTH
1D	2S
3H	4C
4NT	5H
5NT	6H
6S	NB (?)

The key to reaching 7S was North's 5NT bid, which confirmed that the partnership held all the aces and indicated at the same time an interest in the grand slam. If South had looked once more at her hand she could easily have discovered that there could not be any losers after North's aggressive efforts.

And here is a third example from the same event:

NORTH ♠ Q, 7, 5
♥ A, K, Q, 7, 6, 5
♦ 2
♣ A, 10, 9

SOUTH ♠ A, K, 10, 4, 3, 2
♥ 4, 3, 2
♦ J, 3
♣ J, 4

Bidding:

NORTH	SOUTH
2H	2S
3S	4S
NB	

Once more South was lazy. Although she had no controls outside spades she could have encouraged further action by simply bidding 5S, and North, with controls in both minor suits, would certainly have accepted the invitation.

Until then we had an eighty per cent slam record, but the pressure of leading through such a long and important event may have disturbed our judgement at a crucial point.

Slams should not be bid on hopes. You are supposed to bid a small slam even though it depends on a finesse or a break, but you must never bid a grand slam unless you can practically count the thirteen tricks in your combined hands. Here I can tell you a sad tale to illustrate my point.

Mrs Gordon and I teamed up with two of our best young British players during a multiple team event, and we could easily have won but for a few disasters in the bidding. We had to play twenty-one four-board matches, scoring 2 points per board and on the aggregate swing up to 6 points. Therefore each adverse swing could be costly.

On the following hand our team-mates reached 6H while our opponents stopped in 5D and made 6D.

	NORTH	♠	Q
		♡	K, 5, 2
		◇	A, J, 10, 6, 5, 4, 2
		♣	10, 6

WEST	♠	A, 6, 4, 3, 2	EAST	♠	J, 10, 9, 8, 5
	♡	J, 10, 9, 4		♡	8
	◇	Q, 7		◇	9, 3
	♣	Q, J		♣	K, 7, 5, 3, 2

	SOUTH	♠	K, 7
		♡	A, Q, 7, 6, 3
		◇	K, 8
		♣	A, 9, 8, 4

After the lead of the queen of clubs, our partners in 6H had to lose 100 points (2 down). In spite of their clever arguments I still disagree with them; I maintain that 5D or 4H is the correct contract. It would hardly be possible for East to lead a club against 6D, but I don't recommend that contract either.

I don't know why or how, but in a previous match our team-mates didn't reach 6S on the following holding; they just played in 4S while our opponents, who funnily enough used a similar system to theirs, reached 6S very quickly.

NORTH ♠ Q, 10, 9, 5
♡ K, 9, 8, 7
◇ 6
♣ A, Q, 10, 9

WEST ♠ J, 7   EAST ♠ A
♡ 6, 5   ♡ Q, J, 4, 3
◇ Q, 5, 3, 2   ◇ K, 10, 7, 4
♣ K, J, 5, 4, 2   ♣ 8, 7, 6, 3

SOUTH ♠ K, 8, 6, 4, 3, 2
♡ A, 10, 2
◇ A, J, 9, 8
♣ None

Harold Lever gave a good example of courageous bidding on the following hand. It was dealt at rubber bridge in a diplomatic circle, where the stakes were fairly high, and from it politicians and diplomats could learn a lesson in how to take decisions and exercise judgement on a high level. You will see that 6S can be made by East-West unless North leads the ace of clubs and gives his partner a club ruff; but we will never know what North would have led because he did not get the chance. South judged correctly that a cheap save was better than taking the risk of the other side making a slam. His bold action was handsomely rewarded, because he made his contract.

South dealt at game all.

▷

NORTH ♠ None
♡ Q, 8
♢ J, 10, 8, 7, 6, 5, 2
♣ A, 9, 8, 5

WEST ♠ A, K, J, 9, 5, 4, 2   EAST ♠ Q, 10, 8, 6
♡ 9, 3   ♡ None
♢ K   ♢ A, Q, 9, 4
♣ Q, J, 10   ♣ 7, 6, 4, 3, 2

(H. Lever)

SOUTH ♠ 7, 3
♡ A, K, J, 10, 7, 6, 5, 4, 2
♢ 3
♣ K

Bidding:

SOUTH	WEST	NORTH	EAST
4H	4S	5H	5S
NB	NB	6H	6S
7H	NB	NB	Double
NB	NB	NB	

West was convinced that South had bid 7H in defence against 6S and led the ace of spades. As you can see from the diagram there were two leads to beat the vulnerable grand slam—a trump and a diamond. But after the spade lead declarer could discard his losing diamond on dummy's ace of clubs and ruff his two losing spades in dummy. So Lever scored again!

Here is another amusing example. My partner, sitting North, opened 1S and I held:

♠ A, 7
♡ A, K, Q, J, 9, 8, 7
♢ Q, 3
♣ Q, 6

[82]

I bid 4NT. Partner replied 5H; I then tried 5NT, and although she only replied 6D I went to 7H. Trying to find a logical explanation for the final bid, you will agree with me that when your partner has opened with only two aces and one king, he must either have a long suit (in which case he can establish it by ruffing it out) or a solid suit on which he can discard partner's losers. Furthermore the two queens in my hand can play a vital part. But in fact on this occasion there was no problem, because partner held:

♠ K, Q, 10, 9, 3
♡ 6, 4
◇ A, 10, 8
♣ A, J, 2

I have gone round with the hand below to many of the famous, and also to others, but not one person has given me the answer I desired. And yet, if you consider this problem logically the answer seems so natural and easy. You are playing for money (not that it would make much difference if you were playing in a competition) and your partner opens 3H; you next hear 4S; you are not vulnerable and they are. What do you bid on S—10; H—A, K, Q, 8, 7, 6; D—A, 3; C—10, 8, 7, 6?

Four people said, 'I pass'; others said, '6H', '5H' and so on. A few said, 'My partner must be mad, or he has psyched.'

I happened to have held this hand and I did not hesitate for one moment: I bid 4NT. All I wanted to know was whether or not my partner held an ace. A pre-empt bidder rarely does, but if he lacks A, K, Q of his bid suit, it is quite possible that he holds the ace of another.

The bidding in our case went on as follows:

SOUTH	WEST	NORTH	EAST
3H	4S	4NT	NB
5D	NB	5H	5S
NB	NB	6H	NB
NB	6S	Double	NB
NB	NB		

I led a club. My partner returned a diamond, and I gave him a club ruff, so we scored +500.

NORTH
♠ 10
♡ A, K, Q, 8, 7, 6
♢ A, 3
♣ 9, 8, 7, 6

WEST
♠ A, K, Q, 8, 7, 5, 4
♡ None
♢ K, J
♣ K, Q, 10, 4

EAST
♠ 9, 6, 3, 2
♡ None
♢ 8, 7, 6, 4, 2
♣ J, 5, 3, 2

SOUTH
♠ J
♡ J, 10, 9, 5, 4, 3, 2
♢ Q, 10, 9, 5
♣ A

We would have been one down in 6H, but it is almost impossible for opponents to assess the defensive chances in freak hands. Aces and kings do not always produce tricks and when there is a void in hearts there could be a void in spades. The 4NT bid achieved several advantages; for example, West could not tell whether his partner held an ace (in which case 6S would be a virtual certainty). Again, let us assume I had not bid 4NT: our side would never have known what to do over 5S or 6S. Should we push them or should we leave them? The 4NT bid seemed to me a must.

Yet all my bridge friends disagreed. Could it be because their minds were so full of those more complicated methods that their capacity for natural or logical thinking had given way? Of course I did not contemplate that we could make a slam; I only asked for information, which proved to be valuable in the event.

Here is another bidding problem to which very few people find the right solution; yet to me it seems such a natural bid that I cannot understand where the difficulties are.

East deals at game all and opens 4H. Your partner, sitting South, bids 4S and West passes. You hold S—A, 8; H—None; D—A, K, J, 8, 7, 6, 4; C—A, K, 9, 2. What is your bid?

Surely this is a situation in which the only right bid is a grand slam force. This bid (5NT) forces your partner to bid 7S with two of the three top honours in spades. If he has bid 4S vulnerable on, say, S—K, Q, 10, 9, 6, x, x, it is just possible that you may find four spades to the jack in one opposition hand; but it is hardly likely. In fact these were the four hands:

```
          NORTH   ♠  A, 8
                  ♡  None
                  ◇  A, K, J, 8, 7, 6, 4
                  ♣  A, K, 9, 2

WEST  ♠ 9, 7, 3     EAST  ♠  None
      ♡ 5, 4, 3           ♡  A, K, Q, J, 10, 7, 6, 2
      ◇ 9, 5, 3           ◇  10
      ♣ 7, 6, 5, 4        ♣  Q, J, 10, 8

          SOUTH   ♠  K, Q, J, 10, 6, 5, 4, 2
                  ♡  9, 8
                  ◇  Q, 2
                  ♣  3
```

If South had opened 4S as dealer, North should similarly bid 5NT. In either case this grand slam force (which is also called the 'Josephine' convention after Josephine Culbertson) prevents you from reaching 7 if the trump suit is not complete.

This hand occurred in the World Olympiad Ladies' Pairs and illustrates how partners can help each other with logical thinking. West dealt at game all and opened a weak 2S, and thereafter the opposition was silent.

(Rixi Markus)

NORTH	♠	None
	♡	A, K, Q, 10, 7
	♢	A, K, 10, 9, 8, 6
	♣	K, 7

(Fritzi Gordon)

SOUTH	♠	6, 5, 2
	♡	9, 8, 6, 5, 4
	♢	7
	♣	A, 8, 6, 5

The bidding:

WEST	NORTH	SOUTH
2S	3S	4H
	4NT	5D
	5S	6C
	7H	NB

I have never been convinced that the weak-two opening bid is efficacious. It deprives you of the normal strong two-bid; it is not sufficiently high to be of much use pre-emptively; and it gives the opposition a choice of going for their own contract or defending for high penalties.

[86]

Here, over West's 2S, I made the natural cue-bid of 3S. Mrs Gordon, sitting South, responded with 4H. I bid 4NT (Blackwood for aces) and Mrs Gordon showed me one ace with 5D. I now made a grand-slam try with 5S and South had to think this one out. My hearts must be very strong, and her singleton diamond would be useful for ruffing that suit good. It seemed to her that the repeat spade cue-bid probably indicated a void, not the ace. It then became apparent that my worry must be about the one ace that she held: was it the ace of spades or the ace of clubs? Mrs Gordon now found the fine bid of 6C, thus pin-pointing which ace she held and showing some acceptance of my grand-slam try. I hesitated no longer and bid 7H.

What complete confidence Mrs Gordon showed when she accepted a grand-slam try with only four points in her hand! And note that in her thinking she had practically played the hand through.

Next is a good bidding sequence by Rodney Smith and Michael Wolach. It happened during a match against the medical staff at St George's Hospital. There was no inter-ference by the opponents. Dealer South.

▷

NORTH ♠ J, x, x, x
♡ K, 10, 7, x
♢ A, Q, J, 10, x
♣ None

SOUTH ♠ A, x
♡ A, Q, J, 9, 8
♢ K, 9, x, x
♣ x, x

SOUTH	NORTH
1H	3D[1]
4D	4H[2]
4S[3]	5NT[4]
7H	

[1] Not an entirely orthodox forcing hand but strong in distribution and a good fit.

[2] Having forced, it is wise to sign off.

[3] Partner shows further interest and the ace of spades.

[4] Asks partner to bid 7H with two top honours in the agreed suit—hearts.

As you can see, the combined hands contain only 25 honour points but with the help of cue-bids, the grand slam convention and a little imagination by both players, 7H, a par contract, was reached.

Finally I would like to say that this section dealing with slams is a most difficult one; although we know of many conventions which should help us it still happens that even the best go wrong. But there are a few principles which could help those who need guidance. First of all it seems important to fix the suit; next, when you know where you are going, don't jump too fast or too high, but try to obtain as much information as possible without disclosing too much to the enemy. And when you have finally bid your slam, take every precaution and make an all-out effort to make it.

PART THREE

COMMON-SENSE PLAY

Making Contracts

Competitive bridge has overtaken rubber bridge, especially in Britain at this moment. I find it very useful to combine the two games; although tactics may differ they have a lot in common. Crockford's players were lucky, when the club closed down, to be offered refuge at the Eccentric Club in London. Twice a week there are partnership nights when you can play with your chosen partner at 25p a hundred. A special attraction of these evenings is a premium for a grand slam vulnerable bid and made. The following hand is a good example of the Vienna Coup—which happens quite frequently without many players even noticing it.

Mrs Gertie Gottesmann, sitting South, was partnered by Mrs Jane Welsch. Mrs Gottesmann was born in Vienna and this may be one of the reasons why she is familiar with this coup. She was also slightly helped by the opponent sitting on her right, who doubled 5H.

South dealt at game all.

▷

NORTH ♠ Q, 7, 3, 2
♡ A, Q, 8, 7, 6
♢ Q, J, 3, 2
♣ None

WEST ♠ 9, 6
♡ 5, 2
♢ 6, 5, 4
♣ K, 10, 6, 4, 3, 2

EAST ♠ J, 10, 8, 4
♡ K, 10, 9, 4
♢ 7
♣ Q, J, 9, 8

SOUTH ♠ A, K, 5
♡ J, 3
♢ A, K, 10, 9, 8
♣ A, 7, 5

Bidding:

SOUTH	WEST	NORTH	EAST
1D	NB	1H	NB
3NT	NB	4D	NB
5C[1]	NB	5H	Double
5S	NB	6D	NB
7D	NB	NB	NB

[1] Once the diamond suit has been agreed all subsequent bids should be accepted as cue-bids.

West led the 5 of hearts and declarer took the trick with the ace. If the spades break 3–3 there is no problem, but a good player does not rely on good fortune. Declarer got to her own hand with the 8 of trumps, ruffed a club with a high trump, returned to her own hand with a trump and ruffed her other losing club. She then returned to her own hand with the king of spades and played all her winning trumps, producing the following picture:

NORTH ♠ Q, 7, 3
♡ Q
◇ None
♣ None

WEST			EAST		
♠	9		♠	J, 10, 8
♡	2		♡	K
◇	None		◇	None
♣	K, 10		♣	None

SOUTH ♠ A, 5
♡ J
◇ None
♣ A

She next cashed the ace of clubs, on which she discarded the queen of hearts from dummy, and whichever course East adopted, thirteen tricks were sure. According to established custom the lucky winners of the grand slam pool had to offer a round of drinks to the other players, which the two lucky ladies gladly did!

Let us look at a most amusing example of how a master player acts when he finds himself in an impossible contract. Omar Sharif was the unfortunate declarer, and he discovered a most unusual solution to his problem.

▷

NORTH ♠ K, 4
♡ K, 4
◇ Q, 10, 8, 7, 6
♣ 6, 4, 3, 2

WEST ♠ J, 10, 9   EAST ♠ 5, 3, 2
♡ J, 10, 5   ♡ Q, 6
◇ J, 9, 2   ◇ K, 5, 4
♣ Q, 10, 8, 5   ♣ A, K, J, 9, 7

(Omar Sharif)
SOUTH ♠ A, Q, 8, 7, 6
♡ A, 9, 8, 7, 3, 2
◇ A, 3
♣ None

East dealt, and since East-West were playing one of those systems in which 1C requires more points than 2C, he had to open 2C on this hand. The bidding proceeded:

EAST	SOUTH	WEST	NORTH
2C	Double	5C	NB
NB	5H	NB	6H
NB	NB	NB	

West's wild 5C bid forced Sharif into a decision on the five level. His partner should have realised that this was so and not increased the contract to 6H. In fact I think North might even have risked a double of 5C; but this is not the important issue here. The point is that declarer found himself in 6H and had to look for some way of making it.

West led a small club and declarer made his first trick by ruffing. He knew he needed miracles, but they sometimes happen—just wait and see. Declarer crossed to dummy with the king of hearts and ruffed a second club. He then went back to dummy with the king of spades, ruffed another club, played the queen of spades, ruffed (!) a spade and came back to his own hand with a fourth ruff of clubs.

He now faced this position:

```
              NORTH  ♠  None
                     ♡  None
                     ◇  Q, 10, 8, 7, 6
                     ♣  None

WEST  ♠  None                        EAST  ♠  None
      ♡  J, 10                             ♡  Q
      ◇  J, 9, 2                           ◇  K, 5, 4
      ♣  None                              ♣  A

              SOUTH  ♠  A, 8
                     ♡  A
                     ◇  A, 3
                     ♣  None
```

He played the ace of trumps and the ace of spades. West finally ruffed the spade and had to lead a diamond. Omar sighed, said a little prayer, and played the 10, scoring +1430.

An unusual situation and a lucky result, but when you reach an impossible contract you should try to find a possible solution.

Walter H. Salomon, the city banker, is not a tournament champion but he likes to play with good players, and when you see how he played 3NT on the hand below you will agree that he has taken a few hints from the experts on how to deal with a tricky situation at the bridge table.

South opened 1NT and North raised to 3NT. I agree with this bid because a balanced hand often produces nine tricks more easily than ten even if you find a 4-4 fit in a major suit.

```
          NORTH   ♠  5, 2
                  ♡  J, 8, 7, 6
                  ◇  K, Q, 6
                  ♣  A, 8, 6, 3

WEST  ♠  A, Q, 9, 8, 7          EAST  ♠  6, 4, 3
      ♡  9, 3                         ♡  Q, 10, 5
      ◇  J, 9, 8, 7                   ◇  5, 4, 3, 2
      ♣  Q, J                         ♣  10, 9, 5

                    (Salomon)
          SOUTH   ♠  K, J, 10
                  ♡  A, K, 4, 2
                  ◇  A, 10
                  ♣  K, 7, 4, 2
```

West led the 8 of spades, won by declarer's jack. South could count eight tricks, but the ninth had to come from clubs or hearts. He had also to make an 'avoidance play', ensuring that East did not gain the lead and play a damaging spade through his K, 10. A diamond was led to dummy's queen and a small club followed. East was alert and dropped the 10 of clubs, which declarer won with the king, West false-carding with the queen. Keeping in reserve the possibility of dropping the queen of hearts doubleton, or an end-play with that queen on West, declarer cashed the ace of diamonds and continued with another club. When West followed with the jack, dummy played low, and declarer had now achieved his nine tricks without letting East gain the lead.

Had West shown out of clubs, South's best play would have been to win the club in dummy, cash the king of diamonds and play the ace and king of hearts. If the queen of hearts comes down he is home; if not, he will play West for three or four hearts to the queen and throw him in to lead up to his own K, 10 of spades.

Here is an interesting example of what is known in bridge language as a reverse dummy play. As you will see it is not a bad idea to bid and play 6S: success depends only on the position of the ace of clubs. But after the club lead declarer must start thinking and planning, because he knows by then that the ace of clubs is with East. How can he succeed in spite of this setback? Let us watch him and learn.

	NORTH	
	♠	K, J, 10, 8
	♡	K, Q
	◇	K, 8, 7
	♣	K, 8, 7, 6

WEST			EAST	
♠	7, 6, 4, 2		♠	3
♡	J, 7, 5, 4, 3		♡	10, 9
◇	5		◇	Q, J, 9, 6, 3
♣	Q, J, 10		♣	A, 9, 5, 4, 3

	SOUTH	
	♠	A, Q, 9, 5
	♡	A, 8, 6, 2
	◇	A, 10, 4, 2
	♣	2

Declarer ruffs the second round of clubs, enters dummy with the queen of hearts and ruffs a third club with the ace of trumps (he can afford it!). He then goes back to dummy with the king of hearts and ruffs the last club with the queen of trumps. He has so far lost one club trick but made two heart tricks in dummy and three ruffs in his own hand. Here are the remaining seven tricks:

```
              NORTH    ♠  K, J, 10, 8
                       ♡  None
                       ♢  K, 8, 7
                       ♣  None

WEST   ♠  7, 6, 4, 2        EAST   ♠  3
       ♡  J, 7                     ♡  None
       ♢  5                        ♢  Q, J, 9, 6, 3
       ♣  None                     ♣  A

              SOUTH    ♠  9
                       ♡  A, 8
                       ♢  A, 10, 4, 2
                       ♣  None
```

He now overtakes the 9 of trumps and draws the remaining trumps, discarding his two losing diamonds and one heart on dummy's trumps. He has made sure of his contract, however badly the missing honours and trumps may be placed, by reversing dummy.

You could test your skill as a dummy player on the following hand. Sitting South you have dealt at game to North-South and the bidding has gone:

SOUTH	WEST	NORTH	EAST
1H	3S	4H	Double
NB	NB	NB	

▷

West leads a small spade and you see:

	NORTH		
	♠	Q, 10, 8
	♡	9, 7, 3, 2
	◇	A
	♣	Q, J, 10, 9, 8
	SOUTH		
	♠	None
	♡	10, 8, 6, 5, 4
	◇	K, Q, J, 9, 6
	♣	A, K, 6

How do you play the hand?

It is quite simple. If the trumps are divided 2–2 or 3–1 there is no problem; and indeed it is quite possible that East has doubled on A, J, x of spades and A, K, J or A, K, Q or K, Q, J of trumps. But we do not know he has, and we must try and avoid the disaster that could befall us if East holds all four of the missing trumps. Therefore we must not touch trumps until we have eliminated the spades from dummy; only then can we risk a round of trumps. So having ruffed the first round of spades (on which East played the jack), we enter dummy with the ace of diamonds and ruff another spade. We then cross again to dummy by leading a small club and ruff the last spade. This will then be the position:

	NORTH		
	♠	None
	♡	9, 7, 3, 2
	◇	None
	♣	J, 10, 9, 8
	SOUTH		
	♠	None
	♡	10, 8
	◇	K, Q, J, 9
	♣	A, K

Now we can play trumps. The poor South whom I watched when he played this hand forgot to plan and overlooked the warning of the pre-emptor's bid and East's confident double. He played a trump at trick two and went seven down ($-2000+100$ for honours $= -2100$) instead of losing only -300, which would have been a bargain against the 420 and game that East-West could have made in 4S. These were their hands:

WEST   ♠   K, 9, 7, 6, 5, 4, 3   EAST   ♠   A, J, 2
        ♡   None   ♡   A, K, Q, J
        ♢   8, 7, 5, 3, 2   ♢   10, 4
        ♣   5   ♣   7, 4, 3, 2

Louis Tarlo was faced with a real problem on the following hand. We had just had two unsatisfactory boards, so I decided to go all out for a possible top on this one, dealt by Tarlo, sitting South, at game all.

NORTH   ♠   A, 10
             ♡   9, 8, 7, 6
             ♢   K, Q, 9, 8, 7, 6
             ♣   10

WEST   ♠   x, x   EAST   ♠   x, x, x, x
        ♡   K, Q, 10, x, x   ♡   x
        ♢   J, x   ♢   A, x, x, x
        ♣   Q, x, x, x   ♣   J, x, x, x

SOUTH   ♠   K, Q, J, 9, x
            ♡   A, J, x
            ♢   10
            ♣   A, K, 9, 8

The bidding:

SOUTH	WEST	NORTH	EAST
1S	NB	2D	NB
3NT[1]	NB	6NT[2]	NB
NB	NB		

[1] In pairs events no-trump contracts are better rewarded, so South's bid was perfectly justified.

[2] If my partner's bid was based on a fit in diamonds my hand should prove useful.

West led the king of hearts and declarer took stock. He came to the correct conclusion that he would make twelve tricks only if the hand which held the ace of diamonds had no more hearts; on top of this he had to bring down the jack of diamonds.

He won the first trick with the ace of hearts and played the 10 of diamonds to the queen in dummy. Both opponents played small. He then continued with the king of diamonds, and as the jack dropped, all was well.

You will notice that if he allows the 10 of diamonds to hold the trick he can be cut off by East from dummy. He has to enter dummy with the ace of spades in order to play the king of diamonds; then when East takes the trick with the ace and leads a club, he has no entry left for his diamond suit, in which case he will be held to nine tricks—five spades, the ace of hearts, the 10 of diamonds and the A, K of clubs.

Rodney Smith does not need any introduction as a surgeon, but he is also a most generous and kind-hearted person, always ready to help where help is needed, and an extremely keen bridge player. He assures me that he finds it a most relaxing pastime after a heavy day in the operating theatre, yet he plays most thoughtfully and never forgets an interesting hand. I owe this gem to him.

He dealt, sitting South at game all, and saw S—A, 8, 7, 6, 4; H—8, 7; D—A, 5, 3; C—A, 9, 5. He opened the bidding with 1S. West bid 2H, Rodney's partner raised him to 4S and when this bid came round to West he doubled. Being more modest than most bridge players, Rodney assures me that it was West's double that helped him to make his contract on a combined holding which seemed to have five top losers.

NORTH	♠	J, 10, 9, 3, 2
	♡	A, 10
	◊	K, 6, 2
	♣	Q, 8, 3

WEST			EAST		
♠	K, Q, 5		♠	None	
♡	K, Q, J, 9, 6, 3		♡	5, 4, 2	
◊	Q, 8		◊	J, 10, 9, 7, 4	
♣	K, 7		♣	J, 10, 6, 4, 2	

SOUTH	♠	A, 8, 7, 6, 4
	♡	8, 7
	◊	A, 5, 3
	♣	A, 9, 5

West led the king of hearts and declarer took stock. He assumed that all the missing trumps were with West and he decided that he could make his contract only if West held three spades, six hearts, two diamonds and two clubs. He won the first trick with the ace of hearts in dummy. He then played the 2 of diamonds to his own ace, continued with the 3 of diamonds to dummy's king and played the 10 of hearts from dummy. All West could do was to play a heart or a club; in fact he played the king of clubs. Declarer cashed his two club winners and played a spade from dummy, allowing West to win this trick with the queen of trumps; and again West had to give a trick to declarer. A ruff and discard disposed of a losing club, and when declarer then played ace and another trump the unfortunate West had to supply him with one more present of a ruff and discard for his contract.

I often preach that doubling more often than not helps declarer. Although one has to sympathise with West I must criticise his double, because he should have known that he held too many high cards and that there was hardly anything left for his partner. I am in favour of aggressive and attacking methods, but when it comes to doubling high contracts it is much wiser to show restraint and beware of greed.

Michael Wolach is a Russian Pole (or a Polish Russian). He was born in Warsaw, speaks many languages, fought with the Polish army at the battle of Monte Cassino, works very hard, loves music and could have been a great bridge player if he had ever found enough time. He has done well whenever he has competed, and he and I have won several trophies together—amongst them the Master Pairs, the Portland Cup Pairs, the Gold Cup, Hubert Phillips Cup and so on. He is also a very good story-teller and is much respected in the best bridge circles.

When I asked him how he would have played this hand he found the solution in a flash:

NORTH ♠ A, J, 7, 6
♡ K, 8, 3, 2
♢ Q, 3, 2
♣ 5, 4

SOUTH ♠ K, 8, 4
♡ A, Q, J, 10, 9, 5
♢ A, 10, 4
♣ 6

You are playing 4H in South's position and West leads a trump.

Wolach explained:

'I draw two rounds of trumps. I then play ace and king of spades (there is a chance of dropping the queen). Next I play a club, and when an opponent takes this trick his best line of defence is to play another club, on which I discard my losing spade. If he now plays a small spade I discard a losing diamond and my jack of spades will provide me with my tenth trick. If, on the other hand, East leads a diamond I let it run up to my queen in dummy, and if West plays a diamond I must come to two tricks in that suit.'

It all sounds very simple and logical but how many of us would see it so quickly? Many players find it hard to resist finesses. I try to avoid them whenever I can, and this is a good illustration of the fact that there are often safer ways to make a contract than to rely on key cards being in a favourable position.

This was the full deal:

	NORTH	♠	A, J, 7, 6
		♡	K, 8, 3, 2
		◇	Q, 3, 2
		♣	5, 4

WEST	♠	5, 2	EAST	♠	Q, 10, 9, 3
	♡	4		♡	7, 6
	◇	J, 7, 6, 5		◇	K, 9, 8
	♣	A, J, 10, 9, 7, 2		♣	K, Q, 8, 3

	SOUTH	♠	K, 8, 4
		♡	A, Q, J, 10, 9, 5
		◇	A, 10, 4
		♣	6

It is my rule not to mention the name of a player who does something silly. In this case the declarer was a first-class player who sometimes overlooks the ordinary possibilities: his treatment of this hand is quite typical of the kind of player who wants to show that he is in a class of his own. He was convinced even after the hand was over that he had chosen the right path. It was a hand on which anybody would easily bring home the contract, yet he found a way of going down. I must admit that my partner, Nico Gardner, gave nothing away in defending the hand.

East dealt at game to North-South:

```
                NORTH   ♠  A, K
                        ♡  A, 8, 7, 3
                        ◇  K, J, 9, 8, 6
                        ♣  A, 10

(Markus)                                        (Gardner)
WEST  ♠  Q, J, 9, 7, 6, 5     EAST  ♠  4, 3, 2
      ♡  J, 10, 4                   ♡  K, 5
      ◇  4                          ◇  Q, 10, 5, 3, 2
      ♣  K, J, 6                    ♣  5, 4, 2

                SOUTH   ♠  10, 8
                        ♡  Q, 9, 6, 2
                        ◇  A, 7
                        ♣  Q, 9, 8, 7, 3
```

Bidding:

EAST	SOUTH	WEST	NORTH
NB	NB	NB	1D
NB	1H	2S[1]	3S
NB	4C	NB	4H
NB	NB	NB	

[1] After a pass I considered my hand good enough to jump the bidding.

I did not like leading my singleton. Even if partner held the ace it could hardly beat the contract, because he was not likely to have another ace; on the other hand I might easily kill a diamond trick in his hand. I therefore made my natural lead, the queen of spades. Now, if you are not an expert, just look at the four hands and try and find a way of going down. You will say you cannot; but maybe if you are an expert you will understand what happened, because many experts believe they must look for extraordinary solutions on such occasions. Declarer tranced for a long time and then developed the 'master plan'. He led the 3 of hearts from dummy, Nico nonchalantly played the 5 and Mr X went into a second trance; then he played the 9. I took the trick with the jack and co-operated with Nico: showing no surprise, I led my singleton diamond. Dummy played the 6, partner the 10 and declarer the ace. Another long trance followed; then the queen of hearts was played with great aplomb. I played the 4, dummy the 7 and Nico the king. A diamond came back and we made our third trump trick. I had been left with an exit card, namely a spade. If declarer had taken a second round of spades at any stage I would have been end-played; but he hadn't, so I finally came to a club trick.

To give credit to North, who was also a master player, I must mention that he remained silent. So did we—I was speechless and my partner was too polite to express any surprise. Any palooka (ignoramus in bridge jargon) would have made 4H and an overtrick.

You are playing 3NT with the following hands:

NORTH	♠	J, x
	♡	x, x
	◇	K, x, x, x
	♣	A, x, x, x, x

SOUTH	♠	A, K, Q, x, x
	♡	K, Q, x
	◇	J, 10, 8
	♣	K, x

West leads the jack of hearts. You win and you can count eight tricks: where do you go for the ninth? I suggest you play off all the spades and watch the discards carefully.

This was the full hand:

	NORTH	♠	J, x
		♡	x, x
		◇	K, x, x, x
		♣	A, x, x, x, x

WEST	♠	10, 9, 8, x	EAST	♠	x, x
	♡	A, J, 10, 9, x, x		♡	x, x
	◇	A, x		◇	Q, x, x, x
	♣	x		♣	Q, J, 10, x, x

SOUTH	♠	A, K, Q, x, x
	♡	K, Q, x
	◇	J, 10, 8
	♣	K, x

East has discarded two clubs and one diamond on the spades and West, who had to find only one discard, has let go a club. (A brilliant West would have parted with a heart as if he had a reason to keep clubs or diamonds.) Declarer should next play the king of clubs—and now something strange happens. Let us assume West throws a heart: you should play one more club, and if he now throws another heart you can safely play a heart from dummy. Otherwise you will have to guess the diamond position: if West discards a diamond you can throw him in with the bare ace.

In this way you delay the guessing and you gain more information. Should you wish to play diamonds earlier you must win with the king in dummy, because you cannot afford to let East in to lead hearts. East's discards have indicated a shortage in hearts, because he would not throw away winning clubs if he had a third heart in his hand. 'How could I tell?' a thoughtless player would say; but a careful player watches, counts and very often makes his contract in spite of adverse conditions.

Erwin Rindler's hobby is bridge: he is a hard-working businessman from the United States and finds rubber and tournament bridge relaxing. He also enjoys playing in good company and has reached a good average standard. Here is a hand he had to play in 4H to win a rubber:

		NORTH	♠	10, x		
			♡	Q, 10, 9, 8		
			◇	A, K, 10, x		
			♣	A, K, x		

WEST	♠	A, K, Q, x		EAST	♠	x, x, x
	♡	7			♡	J, 6, 4, 2
	◇	Q, 9, 8, x, x			◇	J, x
	♣	x, x, x			♣	Q, J, 10, 9

		SOUTH	♠	J, 9, x, x
			♡	A, K, 5, 3
			◇	x, x
			♣	8, x, x

West led his two top spades and then a diamond to the ace in dummy. Declarer decided to plan his play carefully against adverse trump distribution. He played one round of trumps and ruffed a spade with the 9 of trumps, having noticed the fall of the 7 on the first round. He then cashed his king of diamonds and played a small diamond, hoping to bring the queen down. But East discarded a club, and declarer (who had only lost two tricks up to then) ruffed and started thinking again.

These were the four hands at that stage:

	NORTH	♠	None
		♡	Q, 10
		◇	10
		♣	A, K, x

WEST	♠	Q		EAST	♠	None
	♡	None			♡	J, 6, 4
	◇	Q, 9			◇	None
	♣	x, x, x			♣	Q, J, 10

	SOUTH	♠	J
		♡	A, 5
		◇	None
		♣	8, x, x

After cashing the ace and king of clubs, he played the ten of diamonds. East ruffed with the 6 to force declarer's ace but declarer discarded a club. East then played the queen of clubs. South now had the count of the hand; he ruffed small and made the rest of the tricks. It looks simple but declarer had to be careful not to lose two spade tricks, one club trick and a trump trick.

American card play is of the highest standard. In this example Edwin Kantar displayed his skill by making a con-

tract which seems unmakeable. South dealt at game to
East-West:

```
                 NORTH   ♠  8, 6
                         ♡  K, Q, 10, 8, 4
                         ◇  5, 2
                         ♣  A, 7, 5, 2

WEST  ♠  5, 4, 3              EAST  ♠  Q, J, 10, 9, 7
      ♡  5                          ♡  7, 6, 2
      ◇  A, K, Q, 10, 9            ◇  J, 8, 6
      ♣  K, 10, 6, 3              ♣  J, 4

                 SOUTH   ♠  A, K, 2
                         ♡  A, J, 9, 3
                         ◇  7, 4, 3
                         ♣  Q, 9, 8
```

Bidding:

SOUTH	WEST	NORTH	EAST
1H	2D	3H	NB
4H	NB	NB	NB

I would like to comment on the bidding first. As a member
of a bidding panel of the *Revue Française de Bridge*, I was
asked what I would bid after 1H by South, holding West's
hand. I replied 'Double'. This hand can be played in a spade
contract if partner can bid spades. As you can see, 3S is unbeatable except with a brilliant defence. With a double, I
never promise certain strength or X cards in the other
major suit, because I do not like to impose special conditions for a double. If I have a hand like West's, in which
case we can play a contract in any of the other three suits, I
double. My singleton heart makes it advisable to look for a
combined holding rather than for a 2D contract, which

could theoretically be held to four tricks. If I push opponents into 4H, only players of the standard of Edwin Kantar will make ten tricks. In fact I would expect to beat 4H 99 times out of 100.

The defence cashed two diamond tricks and then switched to a trump. Kantar played the A, K of spades, ruffed the third spade in dummy and then returned to his own hand with a trump. Having discovered that West held a singleton trump he did not play another round of trumps. He ruffed his last diamond in dummy. West was marked with the king of clubs, so declarer played a small club from dummy and the 8 from his own hand. This was the picture:

		NORTH	♠	None			
			♡	Q			
			◇	None			
			♣	A, 7, 5, 2			

WEST	♠	None		EAST	♠	Q, J
	♡	None			♡	7
	◇	Q			◇	None
	♣	K, 10, 6, 3			♣	J, 4

		SOUTH	♠	None			
			♡	A, 9			
			◇	None			
			♣	Q, 9, 8			

West did the best he could: when he had won the trick with the 10 of clubs, he played his last diamond. Declarer ruffed in dummy with the queen of trumps, but when East discarded his jack of clubs he overtook the queen with the ace of trumps, drew the remaining trump, played the queen of clubs and finessed West for the king. Declarer's alertness enabled him to bring home a contract which looked impossible at first sight.

Terence Reese and Jeremy Flint won the Deauville Champions invitation pairs event in 1969. Eight world-famous pairs play matches against each other and all the results are compared, so that your position often depends on how well the other pairs in your seat do, or those in your opponents' places. Nevertheless it is an interesting event and carries great prestige for the winners. Terence was lucky to make his doubled contract on the hand below, but even taking advantage of opponents' slips requires skill. East dealt at love all:

	NORTH	♠	Q, 9, 7
		♡	2
		◇	Q, 7, 4, 3
		♣	A, Q, 9, 8, 3

WEST	♠	None	EAST	♠	K, J, 10, 3, 2
	♡	K, J, 10, 9, 4		♡	Q, 8, 7
	◇	A, J, 9, 6, 5, 2		◇	10
	♣	7, 6		♣	J, 10, 5, 2

	SOUTH	♠	A, 8, 6, 5, 4
		♡	A, 6, 5, 3
		◇	K, 8
		♣	K, 4

Bidding:

EAST	SOUTH	WEST	NORTH
NB	1S	2H	2S
3H	3S	NB	4S
Double	NB	NB	NB

West led the 7 of clubs and declarer took the trick in his own hand. When you look at the four hands you can see that declarer now took a chance on being allowed by West to make his contract, but as diamonds had never been mentioned he could hardly envisage the danger of a ruff. He played the 8 of diamonds from his own hand, and although it seems unbelievable West did not play the ace: he probably feared that it would clash with his partner's king. Declarer took the queen in dummy and was pleasantly surprised that it held the trick. He then cashed his two club winners, discarding the king of diamonds, and when West failed to ruff, it became plain sailing. Timing his play very carefully, declarer cashed the ace of hearts and ruffed a heart in dummy; he then ruffed a club in hand and another heart in dummy. This was now the position, declarer having made eight tricks without losing one:

	NORTH	♠	Q
		♡	None
		◇	7, 4, 3
		♣	9

WEST	♠	None	EAST	♠	K, J, 10, 3, 2
	♡	K, J		♡	None
	◇	A, J, 9		◇	None
	♣	None		♣	None

	SOUTH	♠	A, 8, 6, 5
		♡	6
		◇	None
		♣	None

Reese now led the 9 of clubs from dummy. East ruffed with the 10, declarer overruffed with the ace and ruffed his last heart with the queen of trumps. All West could make was two trump tricks.

If West leads the ace of diamonds, or takes it at trick two and gives his partner a ruff, the defence must come to two more tricks in trumps for one down, instead of a doubled game and an overtrick.

It is always amusing to watch Camillo Pabis-Ticci, one of the bulwarks of the 'Blue Team'. He plays without showing any emotion, he thinks very quickly and he almost always finds the correct solution. He has, in fact, a quick and brilliant mind. He once proudly told me that his son and young Avarelli are on the way to becoming worthy followers in their fathers' footsteps.

Pabis has a wonderful sense of humour, and although my knowledge of the Italian language is rather poor and his English limited to the bidding language, we often laugh together about the funny side of our bridge life.

I watched him play 4H on the hand below, dealt by South at game all.

```
                      (d'Alelio)
          NORTH  ♠  Q, 2
                 ♡  K, 9, 2
                 ◇  K, 10, 6
                 ♣  Q, 10, 8, 6, 3

(V. Shen)                                    (S. Shen)
WEST  ♠  A, K, J, 10, 6, 4, 3   EAST  ♠  9, 8
      ♡  10, 4                         ♡  J, 7, 6, 3
      ◇  7, 5                          ◇  Q, 9, 2
      ♣  J, 9                          ♣  A, 7, 5, 2

                      (Pabis-Ticci)
          SOUTH  ♠  7, 5
                 ♡  A, Q, 8, 5
                 ◇  A, J, 8, 4, 3
                 ♣  K, 4
```

The bidding:

SOUTH	WEST	NORTH	EAST
1H	3S	4H	NB
NB	NB		

West cashed his two spade winners and continued with a third spade. Declarer was well aware that this play was not intended to help him. He ruffed with the 9 of hearts in dummy and East discarded a small club; so did declarer. He then played a small club. East took the ace and returned a club. Declarer discarded a diamond and, as you can see, all the clubs in dummy were now winners. Now, the main problem for declarer was the handling of the trump suit. He came to the correct conclusion that East held four trumps and that his best chance was to drop a doubleton honour from West's hand. He played the ace of hearts, followed by a small heart to dummy's king, and cashed a winning club. On the next club East discarded a diamond, so declarer cashed the ace and king of diamonds: the queen was bound to come down from one defender's hand or the other. Here you have the picture after declarer had made the 9 of trumps, the ace and king of trumps and three club tricks:

```
               NORTH   ♠  None
                       ♡  None
                       ◇  K, 10, 6
                       ♣  6

WEST   ♠  10, 6, 4, 3              EAST   ♠  None
       ♡  None                            ♡  J, 7
       ◇  None                            ◇  Q, 9
       ♣  None                            ♣  None

               SOUTH   ♠  None
                       ♡  Q, 8
                       ◇  A, J
                       ♣  None
```

After he had cashed his two diamond tricks declarer could pin down East's trumps. Excellent card-reading and a well-deserved score.

At another table, after the same bidding sequence and the same opening lead, declarer ruffed the third spade with a small heart and led the king and 9 of hearts. This was bad timing because he lost a precious entry in dummy. He could enter dummy only with the king of diamonds and East trumped the fourth club. Declarer finally had to give up a diamond trick. Camillo's solution was clearly the right one.

Here is a typical case where declarer took advantage of the information supplied by the 3S bidder. For this reason I personally would have bid 2S. I know even this might help declarer, but he might add a missing queen to my holding—in this case the queen of diamonds—and plan the hand differently. Always remember that the enemy also listens and watches.

Jean Marc Roudinesco, for whose game I have great respect and admiration, does not need any further introduction as a player or as a writer. Here is a hand which he played skilfully in 2S, after a club lead. As you can see, dummy's shortage of entries could create difficulties for declarer. Let us watch him:

```
                NORTH   ♠   9, 6, 5
                        ♥   Q, 8, 7
                        ♦   J, 10, 7, 6
                        ♣   A, 7, 4

WEST   ♠   2                        EAST   ♠   K, 8, 7, 4
       ♥   6, 5, 4, 2                      ♥   K, J, 3
       ♦   A, 9, 2                         ♦   K, Q, 3
       ♣   Q, 10, 9, 3, 2                  ♣   K, 6, 5

                SOUTH   ♠   A, Q, J, 10, 3
                        ♥   A, 10, 9
                        ♦   8, 5, 4
                        ♣   J, 8
```

West led the 10 of clubs. Declarer played small from dummy. East took the trick with the king and returned a club. This trick was taken by dummy's ace. Declarer now played the 9 of trumps, which held the trick, and took one more trump finesse. He then played a small diamond, which was taken by East's queen. East played a club and declarer ruffed with his third trump. He played another round of diamonds and opponents cashed their diamond tricks. When West had won the third round of diamonds with the ace he was faced with a choice of playing hearts or clubs: in either case declarer would lose only one more trick. In fact, West played the 6 of hearts.

This was the situation:

	NORTH	
♠	5	
♡	Q, 8, 7	
◇	J	
♣	None	

WEST			EAST	
♠	None		♠	K, 8
♡	6, 5, 4		♡	K, J, 3
◇	None		◇	None
♣	10, 3		♣	None

	SOUTH	
♠	A, Q	
♡	A, 10, 9	
◇	None	
♣	None	

Declarer played the 7 of hearts, East the jack, and declarer won the trick with the ace. He now played the 10 of hearts and East could do nothing but take the trick and play a trump or a heart; in either case declarer would make his eight tricks. You will now see that if the defenders had cashed their three diamond tricks before playing the third round of clubs, declarer would have missed his chance of shortening his hand in trumps. It was essential that he should come to five trump tricks and two heart tricks in order to make his contract.

A master player has to show his art by inducing his opponents to assist him in his task. These opponents were first-class players and soon realised where they had gone wrong, but at the outset East could not know that declarer did not have the ace of diamonds. He might easily have helped declarer by leading away from his king, and holding four trumps he thought it right to make declarer ruff.

Egmont von Dewitz is well known everywhere. Not only is he one of the leading lights of German bridge; he also loves travelling and he often invites players from England to partner him in interesting international events. He once told me: 'I get on so well with those players from Britain—they know so much more about the game and have more imagination than our German players.' But in reality his one and only favourite partner is the well-liked notary and lawyer from Berlin, Dr Fritz Chodziesner, a frequent member of Germany's national team and an excellent player. He is better known as Chody.

On this occasion they were playing in a pairs event, and although 6C seems the obvious par contract on the hand below, they landed in 6S, which depends on a heart finesse or a favourable lead. Egmont von Dewitz learned long ago that one should rely on luck only if there is no other possibility.

▷

NORTH ♠ J, 9, 8
♡ K, 5, 4
♢ J, 9, 8
♣ K, Q, 5, 4

WEST ♠ 6, 5   EAST ♠ 7, 4, 3, 2
♡ Q, 8, 6, 3, 2   ♡ 10, 9
♢ K, 10, 7, 6   ♢ Q, 5, 4, 3
♣ 3, 2   ♣ 8, 7, 6

SOUTH ♠ A, K, Q, 10
♡ A, J, 7
♢ A, 2
♣ A, J, 10, 9

West led a trump. Declarer took the trick in his own hand and played the 2 of diamonds. West played the 6, dummy the 8 and East the queen. There is no reason for East to play anything but trumps: the return of the 10 of hearts could help declarer if you gave him the 8 instead of the 7. Declarer cashed all his winning spades and clubs and West had to find four discards. East was of no further importance. Just let us watch West's plight when the last club is led:

NORTH ♠ None
♡ K, 5
♢ J, 9
♣ 5

WEST ♠ None   EAST ♠ None
♡ Q, 8, 6   ♡ 10, 9
♢ K, 10   ♢ 5, 4, 3
♣ None   ♣ None

SOUTH ♠ None
♡ A, J, 7
♢ A
♣ J

On the jack of clubs West let a heart go, and when the 10 of diamonds dropped on the ace, South had a complete count of the hand. You might ask why West did not play the king of diamonds at trick two. I could not tell you, but I have learned from my own experience that at the very early stage of a hand, few players understand declarer's scheme. West's play of a small diamond at this point, therefore, seems quite natural: how could he guess at trick two the devilish trap that declarer had laid?

As far as bidding is concerned, I would not recommend ordinary players to copy Harold Lever's style, but when it comes to making some of his optimistic contracts, you can take a lesson from him in how to plan your play, how to think logically and absorb useful information received during the auction. Very few players would open 2C on S—A, K, J, 10, 8, 2; H—2; D—None; C—K, Q, 10, 9, 8, 3; but as he explained to me, 'I was first of all interested to know whether partner held the ace of hearts, and on our ace-showing system my 2C bid would find that out immediately.' The bidding proceeded:

SOUTH	WEST	NORTH	EAST
2C	NB	2H[1]	NB
2S	NB	4S[2]	NB
6S	Double	NB	NB
Redouble	NB	NB	NB

[1] Showing ace of hearts.

[2] Having found a good fit you don't mention your own suit.

Here are the four hands:

NORTH ♠ 9, 7, 5, 4
♡ A, J, 8, 7, 6, 4
◇ J, 3
♣ 4

WEST ♠ Q, 3   EAST ♠ 6
♡ K, 9, 5, 3   ♡ Q, 10
◇ A, K, 9, 7, 6, 2   ◇ Q, 10, 8, 5, 4
♣ A   ♣ J, 7, 6, 5, 2

SOUTH ♠ A, K; J, 10, 8, 2
♡ 2
◇ None
♣ K, Q, 10, 9, 8, 3

West led the ace of diamonds. Declarer ruffed, played two rounds of trumps and entered dummy with the ace of hearts. He then played a club and finessed the 9, which West took with his bare ace. West continued with a diamond, declarer ruffed and after trumping two rounds of clubs he could claim his redoubled slam contract. On the double West was clearly marked with both aces, and a careful declarer should therefore not hesitate to play as Harold Lever did. There is nothing to lose this way and a lot to be gained. Bid boldly but play safe!

Many of us who used to belong to Crockford's or the Hamilton Club (neither exists any more) play now at the Eccentric or the Curzon House Club. Rodney Smith found himself in 5D during a late afternoon game at the 'Curzon'.

Dealer North. Game all:

▷

NORTH	♠	K, Q, 9, 8, 6
	♡	J, 3
	◇	K, 10, 4
	♣	A, 7, 3

WEST	♠	A, 4, 2	EAST	♠	J, 10, 7, 3
	♡	K, Q, 10, 8, 4, 2		♡	7, 6
	◇	J, 5		◇	Q, 9, 2
	♣	5, 2		♣	J, 9, 8, 6

SOUTH	♠	5
	♡	A, 9, 5
	◇	A, 8, 7, 6, 3
	♣	K, Q, 10, 4

The bidding had gone:

NORTH	EAST	SOUTH	WEST
1S	NB	2D	2H
3D	NB	3H	Double
3S[1]	NB	4C	NB
4D	NB	5D	NB
NB	NB		

[1] North decided to ignore the double and to rebid his five-card suit.

It is difficult to keep out of game on this hand in spite of three top losers, because neither North nor South can tell that the spade suit is nearly wasted. How did Rodney make not only eleven, but twelve tricks? By a perfect example of timing combined with card-reading.

West led the king of hearts, East petered, and declarer took the trick with the ace. West was marked with at least six hearts for his vulnerable overcall, and when declarer now cashed two rounds of trumps he was glad to see that

West followed. Now the clubs had to be brought into the front line in order to discard a heart from dummy and on the surface it looked as though the clubs needed to be divided 3–3. But see what happens if this is so: declarer plays four rounds, duly discarding dummy's last heart, but East ruffs with his queen and leads a heart and dummy's ruffing entry to the spades is removed. West can now cash another heart when in with the ace of spades. Declarer, therefore, had to hope that the clubs were divided 2–4 with East holding C—J, x, x, x and the queen of diamonds. Play continued with king of clubs and a low club to the ace; the 10 was finessed and then the last club cashed and dummy's heart discarded. Now it was time to lead a spade towards dummy. West did not rise with the ace so the king won. Declarer now ruffed a spade, ruffed a heart, ruffed another spade—felling West's ace—and threw the lead to East with the queen of diamonds. At this stage East held only the jack of spades so he had to give dummy the twelfth trick with the queen.

Do you believe in miracles? I do, but not when I play bridge. This is another good example showing that by using your bridge brain you can win where others lose.

Defence

Defence is definitely the toughest department of the game. Although we now have a few good books about defence—especially Kelsey's *Killing Defence*—the biggest errors are still committed in that department. Below is a hand where I benefited from a slip by an excellent player.

	NORTH	♠	x, x
		♡	K, 7, 5
		♢	A, K, J, 9, 8
		♣	Q, x, x

WEST	♠ A, 9, x, x	EAST	♠ Q, 10
	♡ Q, J, 8, 3, 2		♡ 10, 6
	♢ 10, x		♢ x, x, x, x
	♣ x, x		♣ J, 10, x, x, x

(Rixi Markus)

	SOUTH	♠	K, J, 8, x, x
		♡	A, 9, 4
		♢	Q, x
		♣	A, K, x

Bidding:

NORTH	EAST	SOUTH	WEST
1D	NB	2S	NB
3D	NB	4NT	NB
5D	NB	6NT	NB
NB	NB		

I did not give away much with my bidding, but I am not proud of the final contract. I hoped for a longer diamond suit in partner's hand, and when I saw dummy I did not feel very confident, though I was careful not to show that I had reason to worry.

West led the jack of hearts. This was a cunning lead: if I had held the 10 I might easily have gone wrong. I decided to play for a favourable spade position—namely A, Q, x on my right. Winning the first trick in dummy I led a small spade. The 10 came from East and West took the jack with the ace. He obviously placed me with K, Q, J, x, x, or K, Q, J, x, x, x; but whatever my holding was I do not think that he should have played the ace. He switched to a small diamond and I now decided to play for my only remaining chance—a Vienna Coup. For this to succeed the cards had to be placed exactly as they were. So once again I succeeded because I refused to admit defeat: as long as there is a chance one must play for it.

I cashed the ace of hearts, and when East dropped the 10 I felt much better. I then cashed the diamonds and the clubs, and when it came to the last three tricks this was the interesting picture:

	NORTH		
	♠	x	
	♡	7	
	♢	K	
	♣	None	

WEST			EAST	
♠	9, x		♠	Q
♡	Q		♡	None
♢	None		♢	None
♣	None		♣	J, 10

	SOUTH	
	♠	K, 8
	♡	9
	♢	None
	♣	None

I now played the king of diamonds. East's discard was unimportant. I discarded the 9 of hearts and West had the choice of two evils: whichever he chose my twelve tricks were assured.

A most unusual defence situation arose during a rubber

bridge hand when I partnered one of the most charming French players, Leon Schalit. Although he is not considered of world class, Schalit is a most efficient player and has scored many successes—especially the winning of the Cutty Sark-Queen Tournament with young Bergheimer in Paris at Christmas 1970. We usually meet at the lovely Park Hotel, Waldhaus Flims, in Switzerland, where I go for a holiday in early August. During this holiday I am always determined not to play bridge, but. . . . can you resist when three good friends beg you to make up a game, just for a short while? Erwin Rindler from New York and Dr Chodziesner from Berlin completed the international scene.

South dealt and became declarer in 4H.

	NORTH	♠	J, 9, 8, 7, 6
		♡	A, K, Q
		◇	K, 7, 3
		♣	Q, 2

(Schalit)					(Markus)
WEST ♠ A, 5, 4, 2			EAST ♠	K, Q	
♡ 4, 2			♡	J, 10, 3	
◇ 10, 6, 2			◇	Q, J, 9, 8, 4	
♣ K, J, 6, 3			♣	7, 5, 4	

	SOUTH	♠	10, 3
		♡	9, 8, 7, 6, 5
		◇	A, 5
		♣	A, 10, 9, 8

The bidding:

SOUTH	WEST	NORTH	EAST
NB	NB	1S	NB
2H	NB	3H	NB
4H	NB	NB	NB

Declarer had a problem after the lead of a diamond by West. He decided to try and establish the spade suit, as he had several entries in dummy; he therefore won the first trick in his own hand and played a small spade. West played small and I took the trick with the king in order to let my partner know that I held only two spades; then I played the queen of spades. My best chance to get partner in seemed to be to play a club. Declarer played small and my partner got my message: he returned a spade and I made my jack of trumps for one down.

If declarer had chosen to play immediately a small club towards dummy's queen, West would have had to under-lead the ace of spades and then overtake the second round of spades to give me the same opportunity of making a trump trick.

Here is a hand from a recent pairs event at Juan-les-Pins on which I was let off the hook by the defence. When declarer obviously has no loser in two suits, the defence must force him into losers in trumps as well as in the remaining side suit; but too many defenders give up too easily. South dealt at game all.

	NORTH	
♠	10, 3	
♡	A, Q, 6, 4	
◇	A, Q, J, 8, 3	
♣	10, 5	

WEST			EAST	
♠	K, 8, 5, 4		♠	9, 2
♡	8		♡	J, 10, 5, 3, 2
◇	9, 6, 4		◇	7, 5, 2
♣	K, Q, J, 9, 4		♣	A, 7, 6

	SOUTH	
♠	A, Q, J, 7, 6	
♡	K, 9, 7	
◇	K, 10	
♣	8, 3, 2	

I opened the bidding, sitting South, with 1S; West made a 'match-point' overcall of 2C and my partner bid 2D. Over my rebid of 2S North tried 3H, hoping that I could settle for 3NT, but the best I could do was reluctantly to support her diamonds, so she settled for 4S.

West led the king of clubs and East encouraged with the 7. He won the next club lead and switched to a trump. I played low and the 10 won in dummy. It looked to me as though the spade finesse was right, but I didn't trust this Greek gift—after all, West had come into the bidding vulnerable on a club suit missing the ace, so it seemed only too likely that he had the king of spades, and a losing finesse now would give the opposition the chance to cash their third club trick.

As the cards lay I could, of course, have ruffed a club in dummy, but I wasn't sure that East held another club; so I played the ace of trumps to cut down the likelihood of an adverse ruff and cashed three diamond tricks, discarding a club from my own hand. I was now home and dry.

East should have realised that the only hope for the defence was to weaken my trump suit. If he leads a third club immediately after winning the second trick, I have to ruff in dummy and this alters the tempo. I cannot afford to play the ace of spades, dropping the 10 in dummy; and if instead I finesse the 10 to the king of spades, a fourth club can be ruffed by East's precious 9 and the 8 promoted for his partner.

Whenever a defender has a highish 'useless' trump he should look for ways to promote a possible trump in partner's hand.

Here is a hand which proves one of my favourite slogans: if you try hard enough you can often beat contracts which seem, as they say, 'cold'. Never give in.

On this occasion I opened 1S in third position. South doubled and my partner jumped to 3D (after her initial pass this could only be a pre-emptive bid).

North bid 3NT but South made the final bid of 4H.

```
              NORTH    ♠  K, Q, J, 6
                       ♡  9
                       ◇  Q, J, 9
                       ♣  K, 10, 9, 8, 4

WEST  ♠  8                       EAST  ♠  A, 9, 7, 3, 2
      ♡  10, 5                         ♡  8, 6, 4, 3
      ◇  A, 7, 6, 5, 4, 3, 2           ◇  K, 10
      ♣  7, 6, 2                       ♣  J, 5

              SOUTH    ♠  10, 5, 4
                       ♡  A, K, Q, J, 7, 2
                       ◇  8
                       ♣  A, Q, 3
```

My partner, Mrs Fritzi Gordon, led her singleton spade. I took the trick and returned the 9—a clear 'McKenney' asking for a diamond. This had to mean that I held the king, because had I held a singleton I would have played it at trick two in the hope of getting a ruff. My disciplined partner duly played a small diamond. I won the trick and gave her a second ruff for one down.

In the other room our team-mates, Omar Sharif and Claude Delmouly, reached 6H through some misunderstanding. Nobody had intervened and West led the ace and another diamond, thinking his only hope was to find a singleton in partner's hand. It did not occur to him that declarer, who gave the impression of not having a care in the world, was missing another ace! Having ruffed the king of diamonds, declarer could discard all his spades on dummy's diamond and club winners, scoring + 1430.

I am convinced that you cannot be taught how to defend contracts. You can be told about leads, about counting every suit and working out possible ways of defeating a contract, but to play inspired defence you must have a special gift for it. I cannot enjoy a regular partnership unless my partner knows how to co-operate in making things as difficult as possible for the declarer. There is no greater satisfaction for a bridge player than to have found the killing lead.

Bidding is simple if you follow certain rules, and making tricks from the play of your own and dummy's hand should not be too hard if you have the necessary values; but defence is the combined effort of two bridge brains, and success in it yields unequalled satisfaction as well as decisive points. Try and beat contracts and you will win championships: everything else is easy.

Consider the following example.

Martin Hoffmann is a great bridge talent. To get to the top he would have to accept the need for discipline; nevertheless I enjoyed the experience of playing with him at Deauville in 1971. We scored well, especially in the defence department.

▷

(Hoffmann)

	NORTH	♠	10, 9, 8, 2
		♡	A, J, x, x
		◇	K, J, 9, x
		♣	x

WEST	♠ Q, 4, 3		EAST	♠ A, J, 6, 5
	♡ x			♡ Q, x, x
	◇ 10, x, x			◇ Q, x, x
	♣ A, 9, x, x, x, x			♣ K, Q, x

(Markus)

	SOUTH	♠	K, 7
		♡	K, 10, 9, x, x
		◇	A, x, x
		♣	J, 10, x

I must first explain the bidding. East-West were game and were playing a weak (12–14 points) no-trump, which is usually good for the opponents. North dealt and passed. East bid 1NT, I bid 2H and West bid 2NT. My partner Martin Hoffmann bid 3H, East bid 3S, I passed, West passed and my partner doubled. Then everybody passed. Before I led West 'knocked', meaning that he wanted to explain something. He then told us that his 2NT bid had been a request for his partner to bid 3C. Obviously my partner's intervention had disrupted communication. (Incidentally, this goes to show how involved bridge bidding has become.)

I led a heart and brilliant Martin returned the jack of diamonds, which declarer covered. We cashed three diamonds; then my partner returned a heart, which dummy ruffed. Declarer now played a club, ruffed another heart and played the queen of spades. I took this trick with the king and gave my partner a club ruff. The thirteenth diamond from my partner forced declarer to ruff with the jack of trumps, so we came to one more trump trick for $+800$.

Claude Delmouly, one of the greatest bridge technicians, did not miss his chance to beat a 5D contract on the following hand. His partner was Omar Sharif, and this hand occurred during the Eight Champion Pairs contest in Deauville in 1971.

NORTH ♠ A, J, 10, 9, 8
 ♡ A, 7, 3, 2
 ♢ 5, 2
 ♣ 8, 2

(Sharif)   (Delmouly)

WEST ♠ K, 2   EAST ♠ Q, 7, 6, 3
 ♡ Q, J, 5   ♡ K, 10, 9, 8, 4
 ♢ 10, 9, 7, 6   ♢ 3
 ♣ J, 10, 7, 3   ♣ A, 9, 6

SOUTH ♠ 5, 4
 ♡ 6
 ♢ A, K, Q, J, 8, 4
 ♣ K, Q, 5, 4

Omar led the queen of hearts. Declarer won the first trick with the ace in dummy and led a small club. East played small and South took the trick with the king. As you can see, if declarer now plays a small club he cannot lose his contract because one club ruff brings the ace down; but South could not see all four hands and naturally tried to get into dummy to lead another club. There was also some chance of establishing the spade suit. He therefore played the 4 of spades. Now follows an example of excellent co-operation in defence by Sharif and Delmouly. Omar (West) played the king of spades, declarer took the trick with the ace and played another club, East won the trick with the ace and by playing the queen and a small spade he promoted a trump trick in his partner's hand. I can truthfully report that not all the master players in the contest found this defence!

Here are two good illustrations of several of my favourite slogans: you will soon see what I mean. My partner was Boris Schapiro and East dealt at game to East-West.

(Schapiro)

NORTH ♠ A, K, x, x
       ♡ A, 10, x, x
       ♢ x, x, x
       ♣ 6, 5

WEST ♠ Q, x   EAST ♠ x, x
      ♡ K, J, x, x   ♡ Q, x, x
      ♢ A, Q, J, 10, 9, 8   ♢ K, 7, x
      ♣ A   ♣ K, J, 4, 3, 2

(Markus)

SOUTH ♠ J, 10, 9, 8, x
       ♡ 9, x
       ♢ x
       ♣ Q, 10, 9, 8, 7

Bidding:

EAST	SOUTH	WEST	NORTH
NB	NB	1D	Double
2C	2S	3D	3S
4D	NB	NB	4S
NB	NB	Double	NB
NB	NB		

Of course I should have been one down in 4S, but in a pairs event − 100 is normally a good result against − 130.

My partner decided that I might not lose more than four tricks in spades, while he hoped to beat 5D.

West led the ace of clubs and East played the jack like lightning: you see, he thought that the 4 would not be high enough to convey his message. Then his partner tried the ace of diamonds. East played the 7 and West continued with diamonds. I could now, after drawing trumps, establish three club tricks, on which I discarded dummy's heart losers, making ten tricks for +590.

Do you now understand why I signal only when it cannot cost a trick? It upsets me whenever partner throws high cards at me—unless it is unavoidable or absolutely necessary. 'I had to show you,' is often the excuse. 'Don't show me because I am not looking,' is my retort. In fact it is much more sensible to show which suit you would *not* like your partner to lead.

On the North-South hands below Jean Michel Boulenger and his partner Henri Svarc reached 3NT, which looked an impossible contract. Yet there are 24 good points with a five-card suit plus three 10s. In fact, only a heart lead destroys any chance of making nine tricks.

	NORTH	
♠	K, Q, 8, 4	
♡	5, 4, 2	
◇	J, 10, 8	
♣	K, 4, 2	

WEST			EAST	
♠	J, 2		♠	10, 9, 7, 5, 3
♡	K, J, 7, 3		♡	Q, 8, 6
◇	A, 5, 3		◇	7, 2
♣	J, 8, 7, 6		♣	A, 5, 3

(Boulenger)

	SOUTH	
♠	A, 6	
♡	A, 10, 9	
◇	K, Q, 9, 6, 4	
♣	Q, 10, 9	

West led the 3 of hearts. Declarer won the third round with his ace and played the diamonds. West made two mistakes. In the first place he should have held up the ace of diamonds, in which case he would have enabled his partner to complete a 'peter' asking for a club; but he was in such a hurry to cash his winning heart that he took the second round of diamonds. East played the 3 of spades on the fourth heart. West should have known that the ace of spades could not run away, but the ace of clubs did, because after West led the jack of spades, declarer won the ace in his own hand and continued diamonds. East was now helplessly and hopelessly squeezed in spades and clubs:

	NORTH	♠	K, Q, 8
		♡	None
		◇	None
		♣	K

WEST	♠	2		EAST	♠	10, 9, 7
	♡	None			♡	None
	◇	None			◇	None
	♣	J, 8, 7			♣	A

	SOUTH	♠	6
		♡	None
		◇	9
		♣	Q, 10

Declarer plays his last diamond and discards the king of clubs from dummy. What is East to do?

The Hamilton Club, opened by Colonel Beasley and Jonkheer van Repelaer in August 1939, was closed on 1st January 1971—a very sad event for all who had enjoyed the wonderful atmosphere of this rubber-bridge club in Park

Lane, where some of the best and some of the keenest bridge players used to join in exciting battles. The general standard was high, the play fast; in fact, in spite of its few weaker players, it was the best rubber-bridge school I ever belonged to. The weaker players could not survive unless their game improved, and gradually most players in the highest-stake game (10s–£1) became very efficient.

One of the many occasions I like to remember was when my friend and partner Dinky Gardner co-operated and we made the maximum number of tricks. It was game all and we were 60 below the line. In such a situation it does not matter whether you have announced that you are playing a strong or a weak no-trump; the score allows you a certain freedom. Sitting East, I dealt and bid 1NT.

```
            NORTH   ♠ 4
                    ♡ A, 6, 5, 4
                    ◇ K, Q, 6, 5, 2
                    ♣ 7, 6, 5

(Mrs Gardner)                        (Mrs Markus)
WEST  ♠ J, 6, 3, 2      EAST  ♠ Q, 8, 7
      ♡ 10, 9, 8, 3           ♡ K, J
      ◇ 8, 7                  ◇ J, 10, 9, 3
      ♣ K, 4, 2               ♣ A, Q, J, 3

            SOUTH   ♠ A, K, 10, 9, 5
                    ♡ Q, 7, 2
                    ◇ A, 4
                    ♣ 10, 9, 8
```

South, who never liked to be deprived of his right to bid or to play the hand, looked suspiciously at me as if to say, 'I know you are taking advantage of the part-score', and he bid 2S. My partner doubled and everybody passed. (South could have doubled 1NT, and after 2D by North it would not have been easy for us to compete any further.)

My partner led the 10 of hearts, declarer played small from dummy and I won the trick with the king. I returned the jack of clubs and a small club, and my partner took this trick and played a third club. I then took stock of the hand and played my thirteenth club. Declarer ruffed with the 9 of trumps and my clever partner discarded the 7 of diamonds. (If declarer had allowed this club to run to dummy's trump my partner would have made the same discard, but declarer would have saved one trick.) He then played the ace and a small diamond, which my partner trumped. She played a small heart and declarer took the ace in dummy and played his small trump, finessing the 10. West took the trick with the jack and played a heart, which I ruffed. At that stage we had made three club tricks, the king of hearts, one diamond ruff, one heart ruff and the jack of trumps. Declarer had made the 9 of trumps, the ace of diamonds and the ace of hearts. This was the situation:

	NORTH ♠	None		
	♡	5		
	◇	Q, 6		
	♣	None		

WEST ♠	6, 3		EAST ♠	Q
♡	9		♡	None
◇	None		◇	J, 10
♣	None		♣	None

	SOUTH ♠	A, K, 5
	♡	None
	◇	None
	♣	None

I now played the jack of diamonds and promoted my partner's 6 of trumps for +800. Of course South bid and played badly, but we took full advantage of his weaknesses.

The famous bridge player and author, Edward Mayer, has often explained that psychology plays a much more important part in rubber bridge than in any other game. If you know your enemy's weaknesses you can score heavily. A part-score gives you a tremendous advantage.

Again, especially at rubber bridge you should keep to a natural style of bidding. In this case we might even have made 1NT, but the fact that we gained 800 had a demoralising effect on our opponents, who allowed us on the next hand to play in a part-score which gave us the rubber.

I find defence the most interesting part of the game. Rarely do I have to trance before finding a lead, and on many occasions contracts which appear unbeatable collapse under heavy and efficient attack by a competent partnership. A difficult dummy play which I have misguessed or misplayed does not worry me unduly—perhaps the declarer in the other room also had a blind spot. If the game is rubber bridge I just hope that nobody at the table noticed that the contract could have been made. But I become very touchy if someone finds fault with my defence.

On the following hand there was no doubt about the contract being defeated but we wanted to extract as much compensation as possible for the missed rubber. West dealt at game and 60 to East-West.

▷

NORTH ♠ A, 2
♡ K, J, 10, 9, 8
♢ x, x, x
♣ J, 10, 9

(Lady Rhodes)   (Rixi Markus)
WEST ♠ K, 8   EAST ♠ 10, 7, 5
♡ A, Q, x   ♡ x, x, x
♢ J, 10, 9, x, x   ♢ A, K, x
♣ A, Q, x   ♣ K, 7, 5, 2

SOUTH ♠ Q, J, 9, 6, 4, 3
♡ x, x
♢ Q, x
♣ x, x, x

The bidding:

WEST	NORTH	EAST	SOUTH
1NT	2H	2NT	3S
NB	NB	Double	NB
NB	NB		

South's bid seems bold but with partner's help he hoped to get away with − 300 or push opponents too high. At the same time he hoped to induce partner to lead a spade. You will see that 3NT can be made by East-West, even after a spade lead, so long as declarer plays the hand correctly by keeping South out of the lead. He must therefore play the ace and king of diamonds, in case South has queen doubleton, and not risk a finesse—he doesn't mind North getting the lead if he has the queen.

Against 3S doubled West led the jack of diamonds, East won with the king and returned the 2 of clubs. West won the queen and switched back to diamonds, which East won with the ace, noting the fall of South's queen. Another club went to West's ace and a club was returned to East's king. By then the defence had taken five tricks and it was time for East to take stock. West would not open 1NT with a singleton, therefore declarer had six spades and two hearts left and there was no hurry for the defence to cash the ace of hearts. The only extra trick to be gained must come from the trump suit and if my partner held K, x declarer could pick up all the trumps without loss, unless I could promote a trump for us. That could only be achieved by leading the thirteenth club. This was the position:

```
            NORTH   ♠  A, 2
                    ♡  K, J, 10, 9, 8
                    ◇  x
                    ♣  None

WEST   ♠  K, 8                      EAST   ♠  10, 7, 5
       ♡  A, Q, x                          ♡  x, x, x
       ◇  10, 9, x                         ◇  x
       ♣  None                             ♣  7

            SOUTH   ♠  Q, J, 9, 6, 4, 3
                    ♡  x, x
                    ◇  None
                    ♣  None
```

You can see from the diagram that whatever declarer does at this stage he must lose a trump trick. If South ruffs the club low West's 8 forces dummy's ace; if declarer plays the queen, jack or 9 West refuses to cover and the defence must come to a trump trick. At the table South ruffed with the jack and Lady Rhodes, in her usual impeccable style, discarded a diamond. This is truly what I understand by co-operative defence.

PART FOUR

SURVEYING THE SCENE

The World Title

The Dallas Aces (U.S.A.) have won the World Championship Bermuda Bowl for the second time since the Italian Blue Team retired. This hand was played at Formosa in 1971 during the final against the French team (the current European Champions). It illustrates a small point in defence that was overlooked by the Americans, and superb cardplay by Svarc for France. East dealt with North-South game.

```
              NORTH  ♠  A, K, J, 10, 4
                     ♡  8, 7, 6
                     ◇  8, 4, 3
                     ♣  K, 4

WEST  ♠  8, 7, 6, 5, 3   EAST  ♠  9
      ♡  None                  ♡  A, K, 10, 9, 5, 4, 3
      ◇  K, Q, 6               ◇  10, 9, 2
      ♣  A, Q, 10, 9, 3        ♣  5, 2

              SOUTH  ♠  Q, 2
                     ♡  Q, J, 2
                     ◇  A, J, 7, 5
                     ♣  J, 8, 7, 6
```

At both tables East opened the bidding with 3H, and the

French East was allowed to play there. At the other table Svarc passed on the South cards, West passed and North (Boulenger) bid 3S, which South converted to 3NT.

West led the queen of clubs, and I would fancy that when dummy went down Svarc didn't rate his chances very highly. However, he neatly fitted every awkward piece into his jigsaw in this fashion. He won the opening lead with the king of clubs in dummy and led a low diamond, finessing the 7 to West's queen. West continued with a spade and the pieces were dropping into place. Obviously West was void in hearts, which gave East H—A, K, 10, x, x, x, x, and had East also held the king of diamonds, he would have been too strong for a pre-emptive 3H opening bid. Declarer won the spade lead in hand and cashed all his spade winners, discarding hearts from hand. Now he played a diamond to his ace, followed by a small one to West's king; and West, with nothing in hand but clubs, could only cash the ace and give a club trick to South, enabling him to cash his fourth diamond as well.

Have you spotted the defensive slip? Try playing the 9 of diamonds from the East hand on the first diamond lead. Declarer must cover with the jack, to West's queen, but now when declarer cashes the ace of diamonds West can unblock with the king, and East has the 10 of diamonds for an entry to cash his hearts and lead a club to his partner.

West also had a chance to beat the contract by simply playing the ace and 10 of clubs. Then declarer can come to only eight tricks before losing five. West may have placed declarer with a certain heart trick and tried to play a passive defence; but East's defence was lazy, because the 9 of diamonds could hardly cost a trick and might help his partner to read the hand.

Again and again one hears discussions of such questions

[141]

as 'Who are the best players in France?', 'Which is the strongest pair?', and so on. To decide such questions one would have to follow the play and careers of certain players for a very long period indeed; even then it would be difficult to pronounce a just verdict because current form plays a vital part in success. But nobody will contradict me when I say that Boulenger and Svarc would always be in the running for the title of the best French pair. They are certainly the steadiest, and for years have been the most reliable bulwark of the French team. I was not there and I do not know—even after having studied carefully *Les Championnats du Monde de Bridge à Formose 1971* by Jean-Marc Roudinesco (one of the players in the French team there)— why the French did not beat the Dallas Aces in the final match. It is certainly true that the Dallas Aces were in great form, but any team can only play as well as they are allowed to play. The morale of a team is strengthened when their errors remain unpunished. After they have got away with murder, they usually produce an excellent performance.

Here are a few examples from this battle in Formosa.

North dealt at game to East-West, and against a weak 2S opening bid Svarc and Boulenger bid as follows:

NORTH	EAST	SOUTH	WEST
NB	2S	3C	NB
4C	NB	6C	NB
NB	NB		

▷

(Boulenger)

	NORTH	
	♠	7
	♡	7, 4, 3, 2
	◇	A, Q, J, 10, 7
	♧	10, 4, 2

WEST			EAST		
♠	Q, 5		♠	K, J, 10, 9, 6, 4
♡	Q, J, 9, 6		♡	K, 10
◇	K, 9, 8, 5, 2		◇	6, 4, 3
♧	9, 6		♧	Q, 5

(Svarc)

	SOUTH	
	♠	A, 8, 3, 2
	♡	A, 8, 5
	◇	None
	♧	A, K, J, 8, 7, 3

After a spade lead Svarc easily made his slam.

One of the American players opened a weak 2D bid on North's hand and South found himself in a horrible 3NT contract, which he could not lose.

Here is a hand which was very costly for the French team. At both tables South was the declarer in a 3NT contract, but while Goldman for the Dallas Aces made nine tricks, the French champion missed his chance.

	NORTH	
	♠	Q, J, 10, 7, 4
	♡	A
	◇	7, 6, 5, 3, 2
	♧	Q, 5

WEST			EAST		
♠	2		♠	A, 9, 8, 6, 3
♡	9, 8, 3, 2		♡	7, 6, 5
◇	10, 8, 4		◇	K, 9
♧	A, J, 9, 7, 3		♧	10, 6, 4

	SOUTH	
	♠	K, 5
	♡	K, Q, J, 10, 4
	◇	A, Q, J
	♧	K, 8, 2

At both tables West led the 7 of clubs. Each declarer played the queen, which held the trick. Now you must count: if the diamond finesse works you will make another eight tricks in diamonds and hearts. If the diamond finesse fails you still have a chance if the ace of spades is with West. It is true that if the diamond finesse fails and West then switches to a spade you may lose 200 instead of 100, but in a team event this difference is negligible compared with a chance to make a vulnerable game. This hand cost the French team 12 IMPs and bolstered the American morale considerably.

The hand below was lucky for the world-champion pair, Jais and Trezel. They knew they were down at that stage and took the right decision to bid a chancy slam. As you will see, on the lead of the queen of diamonds even 4S could be a risk.

```
                NORTH   ♠  Q, 8
                        ♡  9, 8
                        ◇  A, 5
                        ♣  A, Q, J, 10, 9, 5, 4

WEST   ♠  9, 6                        EAST   ♠  J, 10, 5
       ♡  K, 6, 4, 2                         ♡  Q, J, 10
       ◇  Q, J, 9, 8, 6                       ◇  K, 7, 3, 2
       ♣  K, 6                               ♣  8, 3, 2

                SOUTH   ♠  A, K, 7, 4, 3, 2
                        ♡  A, 7, 5, 3
                        ◇  10, 4
                        ♣  7
```

The bidding might be of interest:

	(Trezel)	(Jais)
	SOUTH	NORTH
	1S	3C
	3S	4S
	5D[1]	6C[2]
	6S	

[1] 5D is an asking bid.

[2] 6C shows the two minor-suit aces.

In the event the French pair gained 11 points on this board. Trezel had to play for the king and one club to be on his left after his entry card (the ace of diamonds) had been knocked out. He made thirteen tricks. In the other room the American Ace was in 4S and played safely for ten tricks.

Here is a very unlucky hand for the French. 3NT played by the French North went three down because East led a diamond and declarer played the jack from dummy. In the other room the American South as declarer had no problem after a club lead. This meant 14 IMPs for the Aces.

```
                  NORTH   ♠  A, 10, 2
                          ♡  A, 7, 6, 2
                          ◇  8, 7, 4
                          ♣  A, 8, 6

WEST   ♠  J, 8, 7, 6           EAST   ♠  9, 3
       ♡  J, 4, 3                     ♡  K, 9, 8, 5
       ◇  A, 3, 2                     ◇  Q, 10, 6, 5
       ♣  Q, J, 10                    ♣  7, 5, 2

                  SOUTH   ♠  K, Q, 5, 4
                          ♡  Q, 10
                          ◇  K, J, 9
                          ♣  K, 9, 4, 3
```

[145]

Finally a hand that was a battle between two interesting bridge ideologies: the Canapé type of the Albarran system played by Jais and Trezel (with a few mild variations) and the Standard American ideas of Lawrence Goldman.

As the players concerned are all worthy champions my comments are not meant to belittle their greatness, but only to explain their methods and give my own ideas where I would beg to differ. I admire good performances in all departments of sport, art, music and especially bridge, and if I have devoted this chapter to the champions who fought for the crown at Taipei in May 1971 it is meant as a tribute to their achievement in getting there.

East dealt at game to North-South:

```
              NORTH    ♠  8, 7, 4, 2
                       ♡  A, 4, 3, 2
                       ◇  None
                       ♣  A, Q, 7, 6, 5

WEST   ♠  J, 5              EAST   ♠  K, Q
       ♡  Q, 8, 6                  ♡  K, 9, 5
       ◇  A, Q, 8, 7, 3            ◇  K, J, 10, 9, 5, 2
       ♣  9, 8, 4                  ♣  K, 10

              SOUTH    ♠  A, 10, 9, 6, 3
                       ♡  J, 10, 7
                       ◇  6, 4
                       ♣  J, 3, 2
```

Room 1:

EAST	SOUTH	WEST	NORTH
1D	NB	3D	Double[1]
3NT	4S[2]	NB	NB
5D	Double	NB	NB
NB			

[1] Typical of our aggressive Continental habits.

[2] Roudinesco did not hesitate to bid the vulnerable un-beatable game.

Result: +300 for France.

Room 2:

EAST	SOUTH	WEST	NORTH
(Jais)		(Trezel)	
1H[1]	NB	1NT	NB
2D	NB	3D	NB
NB	NB		

[1] Result: 110 for France.

In Canapé style one opens the shorter suit first, even if it is only a three card suit. The Italians use this method; I do on some hands when I face a problem with regard to the re-bid on the next round, but I avoid bidding suits with less than four cards.

Characters

Some players' characters are an open book at the bridge table. They drop their defences and forget they can be observed when their attention is occupied. They become easy victims to a good observer who can recognise the type.

The Tight-Fist

I am afraid that women are the worst offenders in this respect. I have seen this sort of thing happen time and time again:

	NORTH	♠	A, Q, 8, 6
		♡	A, x
		◇	Q, J, x, x
		♣	K, x, x

WEST	♠ 5, 4	EAST	♠ 2
	♡ 10, 9, x, x, x		♡ J, x
	◇ x		◇ A, K, 10, x, x, x, x
	♣ Q, x, x, x, x		♣ x, x, x

	SOUTH	♠	K, J, 10, 9, 7, 3
		♡	K, Q, x, x
		◇	x
		♣	A, x

The contract is 6S and West leads a diamond. East takes the trick with the ace and returns a low one. South trumps with the 3 of spades. One down!

'How could I possibly suspect, partner?' she wails. Then turning to East accusingly, 'You had a seven-card diamond suit headed by the ace and king and didn't bid.'

This is fairly typical of the lazy and mean female approach. When dummy went down South should have worked out that her trump suit was absolutely solid except for the 3. She can afford the 7. Was it mental laziness or sheer meanness? We shall never know!

The Sado-masochist

This type has two ways in which to punish partner: sometimes he makes a bid which can well have two meanings and when his partner chooses the wrong one he sits back with a

meaningful sneer; sometimes he punishes his partner for
his impudence (no expense spared!) as on this hand which I
watched:

		NORTH	♠	None
			♡	A, K, Q, J, 10, x, x
			◇	Q, J, 10
			♣	Q, x, x

WEST	♠	A, 10, 9, 8, x		EAST	♠	x
	♡	x			♡	x, x, x, x
	◇	A, x, x			◇	x, x, x, x, x
	♣	K, x, x, x			♣	J, x, x

		SOUTH	♠	K, Q, J, x, x, x, x
			♡	x
			◇	K, x
			♣	A, x, x

The bidding:

SOUTH	WEST	NORTH	EAST
4S	Double	5H	NB
5S	Double	NB	NB
Redouble	NB	NB	NB

I would rate that redouble as the most sadistic bid I have
ever heard. Partner had said categorically that he considered
5H to be a better contract than 4S doubled, but South per-
sisted with his spades and redoubled to boot. I won't tell
you what the stakes were!

The Doorpost
This player seems to be permanently deaf to his partner's
bids and will never lead his suit. He thinks he knows better
and after presenting the opponents with an unmakeable

3NT game he enquires naïvely, 'Could we have done better?' 'I did call a suit,' his partner replies. 'But I only had a singleton.' 'Ah, I thought you had a void perhaps,' answers East with a touch of the old acid..

Here is a hand which is typical. A player takes a chance to come in with a bid, risking a nasty jolt, just to make sure of the right lead:

```
              NORTH  ♠  x, x, x, x
                     ♡  Q, x, x
                     ◇  A, K, x, x
                     ♣  A, x

WEST  ♠  x                        EAST  ♠  K, Q, J, 10, x
      ♡  J, 10, 9, x, x                 ♡  A, x
      ◇  Q, 10, x, x                    ◇  x, x, x
      ♣  x, x, x                        ♣  x, x, x

              SOUTH  ♠  A, 9, x
                     ♡  K, x, x
                     ◇  J, x
                     ♣  K, Q, J, x, x
```

The bidding:

NORTH	EAST	SOUTH	WEST
1D	1S	3NT	NB
NB	NB		

West led the jack of hearts, successfully killing both his partner's entry and any hopes for the defence. It can be seen that declarer cannot make his contract without a heart trick, and on a spade lead the defence can set up four spade tricks and the ace of hearts.

The Peacock
The vain player cannot, or will not, accept that he can ever

make a mistake, and we can truthfully say that the male is more prone to this fault than his counterpart. If anyone at the tables dares to point out that his analysis is faulty he will 'show you'.

Admittedly this is a difficult hand, but why won't the Peacock ever confess to a misanalysis?

	NORTH	♠	x, x, x, x
		♡	Q, J, x, x, x
		◇	10, x
		♣	J, x

WEST	♠	K, 10, 9, x	EAST	♠	J, x
	♡	x		♡	x, x
	◇	A, K, x, x, x		◇	Q, J, x, x
	♣	Q, 9, x		♣	10, x, x, x, x

	SOUTH	♠	A, Q, x
		♡	A, K, 10, x, x
		◇	x, x
		♣	A, K, x

South played in 4H, and after the Peacock, sitting West, had found the odd lead of the 10 of spades his contract was unassailable. West, of course, remarked, '4H is always ice cold.' He went on:

'We cash two diamond tricks and East switches to a club. Declarer wins, draws trumps, cashes another club, ruffs a club and plays ace and another spade. If I go up with the king, declarer's queen is good, and if I play low my partner has to give South a ruff and discard.'

'But I unblock my jack of spades under the ace,' said East, gently.

'If declarer had played the ace of spades at trick four, you wouldn't have thought of it.'

I am sure that any good player would wonder why declarer had cashed a top spade before bothering with trumps, and would come up with the right answer: But the pride of the Peacock is inviolable.

The Ethical Genius

The only honest and ethical player—in his own opinion—at the table. He watches like a hawk to discover any breach of conduct, trying to prove his own honesty by suspecting other players of doubtful standards.

In this example from a recent competition an inexperienced novice, sitting West, held:

♠ A, 10, 9, 8, 7, 6
♡ None
♢ A, K, 10, 9, 8, 7, 6
♣ None

South, the Ethical Genius, opened 4H and the innocent bid 4S. North bid 5C and East thought a little and passed. South passed and West bid 5D. 'Tournament director!' called South, and complained that West had taken advantage of his partner's slight hesitation. The players were told to proceed with the game, but by now the inexperienced West was so confused that he allowed his non-vulnerable opponents to play in 5H.

▷

These were the four hands:

```
            NORTH   ♠  K, Q, x, x
                    ♡  x, x
                    ◇  Q
                    ♣  K, Q, J, x, x, x

WEST  ♠ A, 10, 9, 8, 7, 6      EAST  ♠ J, x
      ♡ None                         ♡ A, x, x, x
      ◇ A, K, 10, 9, 8, 7, 6         ◇ J, x, x, x
      ♣ None                         ♣ x, x, x

            SOUTH   ♠  x
                    ♡  K, Q, J, 10, x, x, x
                    ◇  x
                    ♣  A, x, x, x
```

The tournament director advised South that his behaviour did not meet with his approval: he should have waited until the end of the bidding and then called for the tournament director, who would obviously have allowed West's bid to stand because on this hand partner's hesitation was immaterial. When West had bid 4S his hand justified at least one further bid in order to show his second suit.

There is a lot of nonsense talked about partner's or opponent's hesitation, but very few players understand the correct interpretation of the law. For this reason I recommend players in competitive bridge *never* to take the law into their own hands but to call for the tournament director. No player should feel offended or annoyed; on the contrary, we have been taught that whenever there is a case to be decided, however clear the decision may seem, one should not hesitate to ask for a decision from the authority who has been appointed for that purpose.

As Others See Me

I conclude with a few examples of famous bridge writers' reactions to my approach to the game—with comments of my own.

'Machine-gun Rixi' is what José le Dentu calls me. I quote from the *Figaro*, January 1969 and October 1970:

'Amongst the great players of the world, Rixi Markus takes a special place with her individual bidding ideas and her exceptional talents when it comes to the play of the cards. Many of the male players don't understand how it happens that she is often placed ahead of them in the large open tournaments and often finishes at the top, even when playing with different partners.

'Just a simple hand is better than all the explanations to enlighten the public. I was in the press-room in Stockholm when, after the fourth session of the Ladies' Pairs Championship, Rixi asked me, "Would you like an amusing hand?"

	NORTH	♠	K, 7, 5, 4
		♡	J, 4
		◇	A, 10, 8, 5
		♣	A, Q, 3

WEST	♠	9, 2	EAST	♠	Q, 10, 6, 3
	♡	10		♡	A, K, Q, 6, 5
	◇	K, 9, 7, 4, 3		◇	2
	♣	J, 9, 8, 4, 2		♣	10, 7, 6

	SOUTH	♠	A, J, 8
		♡	9, 8, 7, 3, 2
		◇	Q, J, 6
		♣	K, 5

'North dealt at love all and opened 1S. East doubled. What would you say in Rixi's place as South? There is no satisfactory solution. You could redouble, you could say 1 or 2NT, you could say 2H, but none of these possibilities occurred to Rixi. "I bid what I think I can make," she said; so she jumped to 3NT.

'The purists might say that the heart guard is not too strong and that maybe there are two or three points missing for this bid. This is correct, but with Rixi the rules have to adapt themselves to the necessities of the moment and her partner has to do nothing but be understanding. This brutal jump to 3NT brought its reward, as West led the 9 of spades, and after a successful diamond finesse Rixi played a spade from dummy, East played the 10 and South took the trick with the ace. She then cashed her diamond and club tricks, discarding a heart and the 8 of spades. Here is the resulting situation, which gave her an absolute top:

	NORTH		
	♠	K, 7
	♡	J, 4
	◇	None
	♣	None

WEST				EAST		
♠	None			♠	Q, 6
♡	10			♡	A, K
◇	7			◇	None
♣	J, 9			♣	None

	SOUTH		
	♠	None
	♡	9, 8, 7, 3
	◇	None
	♣	None

'Having thus made sure of her contract she played a heart from dummy and the unfortunate East had to lead into dummy's spade tenace. In fact East could never avoid this situation after the original lead.

'Here is an extract from a recent letter from England. It is about a 6H contract which was played at four tables and Rixi was the only one to make it, although K, J, 4 of trumps were over her A, Q, 10, 8, 3.

	NORTH	♠	J, x, x
		♡	9, 2
		◇	A, K, x, x, x, x
		♣	A, x

WEST	♠	Q, x, x		EAST	♠	10, x, x
	♡	K, J, 4			♡	7, 6, 5
	◇	Q, 10, x, x			◇	J, x, x
	♣	Q, x, x			♣	J, x, x, x

	SOUTH	♠	A, K, x, x
		♡	A, Q, 10, 8, 3
		◇	None
		♣	K, x, x, x

'With closed hands you can adopt various lines of play, but after the lead, declarer considered that the best solution would be first to try to get some more information about the hand, and make a few tricks before examining the trump situation. The 2 of diamonds was led and she assumed that it was from four diamonds, so she played a small one and ruffed it. She then played A, K of spades in case the queen dropped. She then crossed to the ace of clubs, discarded her two losing spades on the A, K of diamonds and ruffed another diamond, thus shortening her trumps to A, Q, 10. She then tried her luck once more by playing the king of clubs and ruffed a small club with the small trump in dummy. She then played the jack of spades and ruffed it with the 10 of hearts. At that stage West was left with nothing but K, J, 4 of trumps, and when Rixi played her fourth club he had to trump it in front of dummy and give her finally the two trump tricks which she needed for her slam.'

Le Monde, commenting on the same hand under the heading 'Stronger than Men', said: 'Bridge is considered an intellectual sport and as in all fields of sport the male superiority is unquestionable. Nevertheless, certain lady champions can manage to arrive at the highest level, sometimes through sheer intuition, and fulfil contracts which would have been lost by many male experts. In many cases theoreticians will not agree on how to find the best way to make a difficult contract, especially before knowing the opponents' hands. In fact, thanks to an excellent technique, coupled with remarkable intuition, the famous Englishwoman Rixi Markus made a 6H contract played during a match at the selection trials. . . .'

Edward Mayer, writing in *The Times* about the English Ladies' Team for the European Championships in Portugal, said: 'All are seasoned campaigners and might be described as married to the game after devoting a large portion of their lives to it. Each member has her particular technique, but the most formidable pair are undoubtedly Mrs R. Markus and Mrs F. Gordon, who have played together for more than thirty years. Where the path to victory lies in aggressive bidding, Mrs Markus undoubtedly has no peer. When she lost the Olympiad in 1960 she attributed her defeat by the United Arab Republic to their having stolen a leaf out of her book by opening the bidding several times with as few as nine or ten points irrespective of vulnerability and achieving a good result on each occasion. She has the uncanny gift of intimidating her opponents by creating what I can only describe as a tension at the table which upsets their trained or intuitive judgement.

'An example of the devastating position in which her opponents can find themselves occurred in a crucial deal ten years ago when Mrs Markus was South and endeavouring to restore the fallen fortunes of her side. East-West game; dealer North.

NORTH	♠	A, K, Q, J, 7, 2
	♡	7
	♢	6, 5
	♣	10, 8, 6, 3

WEST	♠	8, 6, 5, 4	EAST	♠	3
	♡	None		♡	6, 4, 3
	♢	A, J, 10, 9, 4, 3		♢	K, 8, 7, 2
	♣	7, 4, 2		♣	A, K, Q, J, 5

SOUTH	♠	10, 9
	♡	A, K, Q, J, 10, 9, 8, 5, 2
	♢	Q
	♣	9

'Bidding:

NORTH	EAST	SOUTH	WEST
1S	2C	4NT	5C
Double	NB	6H	Double
NB	NB	Redouble	NB
NB	NB		

'Except through some intuitive conviction that the contract of 6H must fail, West had no reason to double, or, for that matter, to bid 5C over South's Blackwood 4NT, which asked for aces. Perhaps she deduced from North's double of 5C that one, at least, of her opponents did not believe in South's slam aspiration, and she wished to warn East against making a saving bid of 7C.

'Undeterred by South's redouble and relying upon East to produce at least one trick in defence, West passed and led the ace of diamonds; she was happy to see her partner's 8 of diamonds and South's queen of diamonds which she took to be a false card. A second diamond, and not a club, was led and it then only remained to agree the score.

'East could scarcely be blamed for signalling to the ace of diamonds with a high diamond, for how could she credit her partner's raise to 5C with three cards only of her suit?

'As for West, she should have known better than to double the slam without either a trick in trumps or more knowledge of the distribution. The opposing pair at the other table played in what is often described as the correct contract of 5H; so the British team gained 1,120 points on the deal.

'After the match Mrs Markus was invited in a friendly way to explain why she had bid the slam when she was almost certain that there were two aces against her. Her answer was typical of her ruthless outlook: "I had no idea what my partner's double of 5C meant—especially since East would have made the contract with an overtrick. I simply could not resist the chance of a slam, so I not only bid it but redoubled."

'Although I should like to describe the result as exceptionally lucky, she was really giving a superb example of fine judgement in a tight situation where her opponents failed to rise to the occasion.'

Careful analysis will indeed show that East-West could have made a slam in either clubs or diamonds.

In his book, *Bridge Facile*, José le Dentu quotes a hand

which occurred during the European Championships in Baden-Baden in 1963, where the British Ladies won the title. The same team became Olympic Champions in 1964 in New York.

'World champion Rixi Markus is an exceptional player; her direct and courageous approach to bidding have made her famous. There is no-one else who knows how to finish at the top in the strongest and largest fields with many different partners. . . .

'Here is a typical example of her bidding style and the way she plays safe to make her contract even against adverse conditions. Dealer South. East-West game; Rixi Markus South.

NORTH	♠	Q, 9, 3
	♡	7, 6, 4
	◇	A, 7, 3
	♣	K, 8, 5, 2
SOUTH	♠	A, K, J, 10
	♡	A, 9, 8
	◇	K, Q, 10, 9, 8, 5
	♣	None

Bidding:

SOUTH	NORTH
2D	3D[1]
3H[2]	3NT[3]
4S[4]	5D
6D	NB

[1] Shows an ace and fixes the suit.

[2] Hoping to stop a heart lead.

[3] Shows a balanced hand and should be taken as a sign-off.

[4] She is not put off.

'West led a diamond and here is the full hand. You can see how Rixi gave herself more than one chance.

	NORTH	
	♠	Q, 9, 3
	♡	7, 6, 4
	◇	A, 7, 3
	♣	K, 8, 5, 2

WEST			EAST		
♠	8, 2		♠	7, 6, 5, 4
♡	K, 10, 5, 2		♡	Q, J, 3
◇	4		◇	J, 6, 2
♣	A, 10, 7, 6, 4, 3		♣	Q, J, 9

	SOUTH	
	♠	A, K, J, 10
	♡	A, 9, 8
	◇	K, Q, 10, 9, 8, 5
	♣	None

'She won the first diamond in her own hand and played a small heart, which was taken by East, who played a second round of trumps. Declarer took this trick in dummy and played a club (it has been known for a defender to play the ace in such a case, or for the ace to come down on the second round). She then entered dummy with the queen of spades and played one more round of clubs in case . . . and finally she had to rely on her last chance, namely that the hand with the three trumps would have four spades and she could discard her losing heart from dummy and ruff a heart for her twelfth trick.

'In the other room declarer played two rounds of trumps, then a small heart and East could remove the last trump in dummy. Did I say that timing was important?'

Looking Ahead

In recent years accusations of cheating in competitive bridge have become more and more frequent. Why? And how can the situation be improved? Having an inquisitive mind I have discussed this problem with many players and here are my impressions.

The winning of major international competitions carries more important rewards than would appear on the surface. For instance, the team that wins the European Championship is assured of a trip to South America, North America or the Far East to compete in the World Championship. The team winning the World Championship automatically qualifies to defend its title the following year.

Apart from the personal prestige of representing his country, the amateur player's rewards seem small. Although nominally his basic expenses are met by his country's association he still has to pay for a couple of meals a day and various other extras. He is playing or 'on call' from about 1.30 in the afternoon until 1.30 in the morning, twelve days out of fourteen, with several morning team meetings. One could not call this a free holiday. But when one looks at the professional players, columnists, authors and teachers, the picture becomes clearer. The prestige is not now just personal, it is commercial. 'Our World Champion Bridge Correspondent cables the latest results from. . . .' has a certain majestic ring about it; obviously while he holds the title he can command a higher price. Afterwards come the invitations, *all* expenses paid (often with a bonus), to take a team to the Far East, to take charge of a bridge cruise, to enhance the prestige of a tournament, to commentate on *Bridgerama* and so on; none of which engagements need interfere with—indeed they may help to promote—the professional bridge player's normal activities.

To the consternation of the professional coterie the Italians won the World Championship twelve times before they recently retired. They are all amateurs with important jobs and family commitments. Other countries' teams were getting irritable and dispirited at this constant proof of superiority and could not understand why the Italians were unbeatable. The answer is simple: theirs was the best team. Nevertheless it was only natural for some members of unsuccessful teams and their loyal followers in the audience to suggest that perhaps there was 'more to it'—and so the whispers started.

I will quote two well-known occasions. One was at Stockholm in 1956 and the other at the Olympiads during the final at Deauville in 1968. In each case Italy won the title.

North was dealer with North-South game and the bidding was:

NORTH	EAST	SOUTH	WEST
1D	NB	2C	2S
3C	3H	3NT	4H
NB	NB	6C	NB
NB	NB		

Sitting West and holding:

♠ A, Q, 9, x, x, x
♡ Q, 10, x
♦ Q, 9, 8
♣ x

what should you lead?

The unthinking player automatically leads his partner's

suit, hearts. But let us consider the implications of the bidding. South was prepared to settle for 3NT until hearts had been supported by West, and then he jumped to 6C. Why? East had not bid over the opening 1D and could therefore hold little but a string of hearts, so South must have been able to deduce from West's 4H bid that his partner held only a singleton heart. His hand begins to take shape something like this:

♠ K, x, (x)
♡ A, x, x
♢ x, (x)
♣ A, Q, 10, x, x, x

Judging by North's bidding—opening 1D and supporting clubs at the three level with no attempt to play the hand in no-trumps—he should hold roughly:

♠ x, x, x
♡ x
♢ A, K, J, x, x
♣ K, J, x, x

It thus becomes manifest that with West's queen of diamonds in such a precarious position the only real hope of defeating the contract is for both North and South to hold three spades, so that West can give his partner a ruff. In fact the four hands were:

▷

	NORTH	♠	J, x, x
		♡	x
		◇	A, K, J, x, x
		♣	K, J, x, x

WEST	♠	A, Q, 9, x, x, x	EAST	♠	10
	♡	Q, 10, x		♡	K, J, 9, x, x, x
	◇	Q, 9, 8		◇	10, x, x, x
	♣	x		♣	x, x

	SOUTH	♠	K, x, x
		♡	A, x, x
		◇	x
		♣	A, Q, 10, x, x, x

After coming to this conclusion, the Italian West led ace and
another spade and the contract went down.

On the next hand the bidding had gone:

SOUTH	WEST	NORTH	EAST
1S	NB	2H	NB
2S	NB	3S	NB
4S	NB	NB	NB

Sitting West you hold:

	♠	J, 8, x
	♡	x
	◇	A, 9, x, x, x
	♣	A, 9, x, x

What do you lead?

In this case you apply the rule of elimination. A trump
lead would kill a trick if partner held, say, Q, x or A, x. The
singleton heart seems most unlikely to succeed since, in spite
of the stuttering way the opposition reached their game contract, it is reasonable to assume that they hold the other two

aces; so partner's heart guard may be massacred, and the defence with it.

So we are down to a choice between the two minor suit aces. It is possible that partner holds the king of one of these suits; furthermore, if West leads an ace he can, at least, get a look at dummy, which might help with the next lead. Which ace? The shorter suit seems the safer because the ace of diamonds may release too many winners for declarer. So the Italian West led the ace of clubs.

These were the four hands:

```
            NORTH  ♠  K, x
                   ♡  A, J, 10, 9, x
                   ◇  x
                   ♣  Q, J, x, x, x

WEST  ♠  J, 8, x          EAST  ♠  Q, x
      ♡  x                      ♡  Q, x, x, x, x
      ◇  A, 9, x, x, x          ◇  Q, 10, x, x, x
      ♣  A, 9, x, x            ♣  10

            SOUTH  ♠  A, 10, 9, x, x, x
                   ♡  K, x
                   ◇  K, J
                   ♣  K, x, x
```

You can see that as long as West leads an ace and then gives his partner a club ruff the game contract is beaten. The West player at the other table led his singleton heart and was the first to admit his error when discussing this hand afterwards.

On both occasions voices in the audience were heard expressing astonishment at the killing lead, which to top players seemed natural and obvious after a careful analysis.

Experienced players have paid dearly for their mistakes. They have learned that the general rules laid down in the textbooks are not infallible, and they always analyse the bidding to see whether they should deviate from these rules. I would not advise a beginner, or even a more advanced player, to look for 'fancy' leads, but when a champion leads he takes account of the entire history of the hand. He listens to the bidding, he assesses the situation, he knows his opponents and their habits and systems, and his final decision is the upshot of all these considerations. Especially in team events, but also in rubber bridge, the first duty of the opening leader is to attempt to beat the contract—never mind the overtricks at this stage—and what he chooses to lead is likely to be decisive.

I asked Edgar Kaplan not so long ago—and I count him amongst the greatest experts in the world—how he would tackle an accusation against a partnership regarding opening leads. He told me that he would take a fair number (say 80–100) of the hands they had defended and give a good average player the cards held by the partner of the opening leader in each case. He would then ask, 'What is the lead you desire?' If every time the desired lead had been produced he would regard this as conclusive proof that this partnership was using a code for leads.

Many years ago Terence Reese gave me a similar answer when I questioned him. 'If in 100 hands a partnership produces each time the opening lead that suits the leader's partner—not the natural, or maybe the killing lead, but the lead that suits his partner's hand—I would consider that they must have a code for leads.'

In all bridge organisations there are specially selected committees with authority to take advice when necessary on these matters, and on the whole I, like many others, am convinced that all the well-known partnerships are highly ethical. It would certainly spoil the pleasure of any achievement of my own to know too much. I find the game fascinating because each hand is an unknown quantity and a puzzle which I am trying to resolve. If I knew the answer beforehand, where would be the pleasure and the satisfaction?

Increased bridge activities all over the world have produced an entirely new picture. The organisations have grown so rapidly that it must be a heavy task for those who run a nation's bridge life to cope with all the mounting difficulties efficiently. I can only find words of praise and admiration for the 'men at the top'. Nevertheless, looking at it from the angle of the individual competitor, or even the ordinary player, I feel that some needs have been grossly neglected. The fact that the players themselves are not represented when it comes to important decisions which will influence their progress in their bridge careers indicates that there is something wrong somewhere.

Selection methods in most countries have been criticised, and it is probably impossible to find a method which will please everybody. Those who are chosen rarely complain; those who have been left out try to air their grievances. But it seems to me that there should be more understanding at the top for the performers. It would be going too far to say that we should have a union to represent us, but I found it incredible, for instance, when in 1970, with only three teams entering for the selection trials for the European Championship in Estoril—on which occasion my team, consisting of four players, won 45 out of 48 possible victory points—we were not consulted as to the choice of the third pair. There was, unfortunately, not much to choose from in that year. Several new experimental partnerships were tried out.

Nevertheless there were two experienced pairs, and as it is most important that a team should consist of six players who are in tune and who get on well together, we might have suggested that one of these two pairs should be chosen. As soon as a disturbing element is brought into the team its chances of winning are destroyed.

Then there is the question of captaincy. It is the practice in many countries to appoint a captain without consulting the team, although it may be detrimental to the team to do so. How can a team function well if there is not a harmonious relationship between the captain and its members? It has been shown again and again that a good captain is much more likely to lead his team to victory. Of course there are such things as bridge politics; there are bridge intrigues; there is string-pulling. Some of these things may be unavoidable, but generally speaking more co-operation and more discussion between the players and the autocrats who run the country's bridge life should be offered to the candidates.

We are now in a ridiculous position in Britain because some strange interpretation of the Gaming Law classifies bridge as a game of chance, and a bridge host or hostess as a croupier, who is not allowed to take part in the game. I do not know what stupidity led to this interpretation, because anyone who understands what bridge is about knows that a host or hostess is often essential to complete a bridge four or bridge eight. In London most bridge centres and bridge clubs have been forced to close down because of these anomalies. Visitors from abroad ask me again and again, 'Where can I play bridge in London?', and believe me it is not easy to find a place where you can enjoy a pleasant game. You are either tucked away in a corner at some gaming casino or you are waiting for a fourth because the host or hostess is not allowed to participate. It seems that there are not enough bridge players in the House of Commons.

There is also a general lack of radio or television interest in bridge—and a neglect in newspaper reporting of national triumphs. As I said to the Press—and they were there in force—when Reese and Schapiro returned from the Argentine, 'When there is a scandal or unpleasant incident you come with all your cameras and reporters, but when we bring home World Championship trophies, you are conspicuously absent.' Not that I am seeking publicity, but Britain as a country has done exceedingly well in international and world bridge, and believe me, it is hard work to win those contests. The competition is very tough and it would be much more encouraging to know that at home there was some interest in these achievements.

In America, where bridge is more commercialised as it is a vast country and has huge resources, bridge teachers and bridge writers are highly paid, to which I often remark, 'Here we do things mostly for love, and there mostly for money.' I am not in favour of turning bridge into an entirely professional sport but different countries have different attitudes. The rewards have become increasingly high for those who are well placed. We can compare it in a way to golf competitions. In recent years bridge has become much more a spectator's game, thanks to the possibility of projecting the play on either *Bridgerama* or *View-Graph*, and discussing it with the audience participating. This is a special feature at the *Guardian* Easter Tournament, and also abroad at big festivals.

I do not think that we can stop the development and progress of international bridge life and bridge relations, nor is there any reason why one should wish to do so while the game is gaining popularity all over the world and attracting new recruits, but the organisers should not neglect to consider some of the consequences of this new turn of events. I find it wrong, for instance, that world and international events should take place in cities or countries which are too expensive for some who would like to compete. We should either try to get more favourable terms when a venue is chosen, or choose only those places which can offer us more favourable conditions. Bridge is probably the one sport where different nations and creeds get together and forget their differences whilst enjoying a game against each other.

In spite of the official attitude of the Egyptian Government—that no Egyptian team should play against an Israeli one—I have been present when Lebanese and Egyptian players, as well as players from other Arab countries, have sat down in a most friendly fashion to play in competition against Israel. Bridge can build bridges for international understanding. We also welcome competitors from Communist countries. When Warsaw staged the European Championship in 1966 we were received with warmth and courtesy and the championship was much enjoyed by all who took part. This year (1971) we are going to Greece and I am sure that in spite of differences in political ideas we shall all find a way to be friends and create an atmosphere of understanding, and shall express our desire for peace and goodwill in international bridge terms.

We are still waiting for Russia and China to join us, but the World Federation has done a wonderful job so far and the membership grows steadily. It is our duty as writers and columnists to spread the gospel.